Transformation
—Change Begins Within—

The Journey To Your Best Self

Dr. Lee A. Simpson

Published by:

DLS Creativeworks, LLC

Amarillo, TX

Scripture quotations, unless otherwise noted, are from the New King James Version (NKJV). Copyright © 1982 by Thomas Nelson, Inc. Used by permission. All rights reserved.

This book is a work of nonfiction. Every effort has been made to ensure the accuracy of information and scripture references. Any resemblance to actual persons, living or dead, is purely coincidental.

ISBN: 979-8-9913425-0-6

Cover Design by: DLS Creativeworks

Interior Design by: LifeBooks

Printed in the United States of America

First Edition: 2024

DEDICATION

To every seeker of growth, hope, and renewal—this book is dedicated to you, the courageous soul who dares to embrace change, confront challenges, and pursue the journey to becoming your best self.

To those who have faced setbacks yet rise again, to those who carry dreams in their hearts and trust in God's timing, and to those who yearn for a life aligned with purpose and meaning—may you find encouragement, inspiration, and strength within these pages.

And above all, to the One who makes transformation possible—our Creator, Redeemer, and Sustainer—may all glory and honor be Yours, Lord, as we align our lives with Your purpose and walk the path You have set before us.

With faith, hope, and love,

Dr. Lee A. Simpson

CONTENTS

Preface   VII

Introduction   IX

1. Transformation: My Story   1

2. What is Change?   7

3. The Forged: The Forces of Change   15

4. The Four Pillars of Change   23

5. Understanding Transformation   35

6. A Portrait of Grace: A Man Named Zacchaeus   41

7. A New Heart, A New You   51

8. Metamorphosis: The Parallel Between A Caterpillar, A   57
    Butterfly And Believers - Pt. 1

9. The Power of Choice   61

10. Indecision: The Silent Thief of Dreams and Opportunities   69

11. Success Stories of Modern-Day Christians Who Overcame   81
    Indecision

12. Decisiveness: The Power of A Made-Up Mind   87

13. Renewing the Mind: The Foundation of Transformation   99

14. The Battle of The Mind: Anxiety, Depression, And Stress   105

15. Biblical Meditation   113

16. Exploring Our Default Patterns   119

17. How To Break Negative Behavior Patterns   133

18. The Dangers of Unhealed Emotional Trauma   145

19. Overcoming "Negative 'Self-Talk'   155

20. The Story of Jabez   161

21. The Role Of Repentance In Personal Growth   173

22. The Transformative Impact of Self-Awareness   183

23. Personal Development: A Journey of Faith and Growth   189

24. Developing A Success Mindset   199

25. Understanding Your "Why": The Foundation for Purpose-   209
    ful Living

26. Metamorphosis: The Parallel Between A Catapilla, A But-   213
    terfly and Believers - Pt. 2

27. The Trifecta Of Transformation: Desire, Decision, And   221
    Discipline

28. The Journey to Your Best Self   229

29. Transformation: Your Journey to a New You   235

Acknowledgements   239

Connect With The Author   240

PREFACE

Life often feels like a relentless cycle of struggle and longing. For so many, the desire to change and grow seems just out of reach, trapped beneath the weight of repeated failures, deeply ingrained habits, and a mind overwhelmed by fear, anxiety, or despair. If you've ever found yourself wondering, *"Why can't I change? Why does transformation seem impossible?"*—this book is for you.

The truth is, true transformation isn't about trying harder; it's about aligning with a higher purpose and power. As the Apostle Paul wrote in Romans 12:2, "Be transformed by the renewing of your mind." Lasting change begins within. It's not about willpower alone but about partnering with God to reframe our thoughts, break the chains of negative patterns, and step into a life of freedom and purpose.

The world today is gripped by an epidemic of anxiety, depression, and stress. Many are searching for peace in all the wrong places—self-help fads, fleeting pleasures, or the distractions of modern life. Yet, the Bible offers a timeless, life-changing solution. Through the Word of God, we discover principles to combat anxiety, heal brokenness, and restore joy. This book doesn't offer a quick fix or empty platitudes; instead, it provides a roadmap to renewal, rooted in Scripture and grounded in practical steps.

The journey to your best self isn't about perfection—it's about progress. Throughout these pages, we'll explore how to harness the power of the Holy Spirit to overcome obstacles and how to adopt a mindset that reflects

God's truth about who you are and what you can become. This book isn't just for the believer who feels stagnant but also for the seeker who longs for a breakthrough.

Each chapter is designed to address key areas of transformation, drawing on the principles outlined in the Table of Contents (T.O.C.) to guide you step by step:

- How to conquer limiting beliefs and embrace God's promises

- Strategies to renew your mind and cultivate godly habits

- A Biblical approach to managing anxiety, depression, and stress

- Real-life stories and case studies of those who found freedom through God's power

This isn't just a book—it's an invitation to a journey. You'll be challenged to reflect, pray, and act. Transformation is not passive; it requires your active participation and a willingness to surrender old ways for new ones. But as you'll discover, when you take even the smallest steps in faith, God multiplies your efforts in ways you could never imagine.

So, are you ready to begin? The change you've been longing for is not only possible—it's promised. Together, let's take the first step toward the life you were created to live.

INTRODUCTION

THE LONGING FOR MORE

Have you ever felt it? That quiet nudge deep in your soul, calling out above the chaos of life? It's like a soft whisper, urging you to step into something bigger, something more meaningful. Maybe you've found yourself wondering, "Is there more to me than what I see right now?" That pull you're feeling—it's not random. It's God. He's inviting you to step into a life of transformation.

This journey, the heart of *Transformation: Change Begins Within - The Journey to Your Best Self,* isn't about quick fixes or just reaching goals. Those things are important, but they're only on the surface. Real change happens deep inside, where the Holy Spirit begins His work in your heart. It's in that sacred place where God reshapes who you are, aligns your purpose with His plan, and fills your life with meaning.

You've probably heard this verse before: *"For I know the thoughts that I think toward you, says the LORD, thoughts of peace and not of evil, to give you a future and a hope"* (**Jeremiah 29:11, NKJV**). But have you truly let those words sink in? They're more than just encouraging lines—they're God's promise. He's been planning your future, crafting your story, and drawing you toward the life He's always envisioned for you.

Over the years, I've had the blessing of witnessing countless lives transformed by God's hand. And if there's one thing I've learned, it's this: lasting change doesn't come from trying harder or rearranging your life on the outside. It starts deep within—with a heart fully open to God. David's heartfelt prayer captures it perfectly: *"Search me, O God, and know my heart"* (**Psalm 139:23, NKJV**). That's where transformation begins—when you invite God into the deepest parts of your soul.

This book isn't another self-help manual, and it's not about striving to become a better version of yourself by your own strength. No, this is an invitation. It's a call to partner with the One who knows you better than you know yourself. Together, we'll explore truths that will unlock the transformation God has already begun in you:

- How to break free from the patterns that keep holding you back

- What it means to let God's Word renew your mind and reshape your thoughts

- The importance of the healing of the heart and soul

- How to build a mindset rooted in God's truth

- How to live a life guided by the Holy Spirit

Uncovering God's Masterpiece

Here's the amazing truth: transformation isn't about becoming someone entirely new. It's about uncovering the masterpiece God has already created within you. Every obstacle you've faced, every challenge you've overcome—it's all been part of His divine plan to shape you for the future He has prepared.

The Bible reminds us: *"Therefore, if anyone is in Christ, he is a new creation; old things have passed away; behold, all things have become new."* **(2 Corinthians 5:17, NKJV).**

This transformation isn't a one-time event; it's an ongoing, beautiful process. God is continually at work in you, renewing you day by day and leading you step by step into the fullness of His purpose.

Are You Ready?

If you've been weighed down by the past, stuck in cycles of negativity, or just longing for more of God's presence in your life, hear this: the stirring in your heart is no accident. It's God's way of letting you know He's already moving, preparing you for something greater than you can imagine.

So, what do you say? Are you ready to answer His call? To step into a life of transformation, hand in hand with the One who created you? If you're ready to take that step, turn the page. Together, let's embark on this journey of faith, discovery, and renewal. The transformation you've been searching for starts right here.

With faith and expectation,
Dr. Lee A. Simpson

CHAPTER 1

TRANSFORMATION: MY STORY

The path to personal growth isn't a smooth, straight road. It's full of twists and turns—moments of joy, frustration, unexpected detours, and even a few roadblocks. No matter how determined we are to change, we often find ourselves slipping back into old habits and mindsets that keep us stuck. We try to fix things on the outside, thinking sheer willpower is all we need to break bad habits, improve our quality of life, find success, grow spiritually, or become better versions of ourselves. But inside, the same struggles remain—unresolved issues, unfulfilled longings, and that frustrating sense of being stuck.

I know what that feels like. Years ago, even as someone who loved God, I wrestled with a persistent inner voice telling me I wasn't enough. I tried harder—thinking that if I just did more or did better, I'd finally experience lasting change. But my prayers seemed unanswered, my efforts felt futile, and I wondered: **Is real transformation even possible?**

The Turning Point

Sometimes, God brings opportunities for change in the most unexpected ways. For me, it happened on an ordinary day while watching a Christian TV program. The speaker was teaching on Romans 12, particularly about renewing your mind. His words struck me deeply—it felt as though God Himself was speaking directly to my heart.

I opened my Bible and read: *"Do not conform to the pattern of this world, but be transformed by the renewing of your mind"* (Romans 12:2).

That verse wasn't just words on a page—it became the starting point of a journey that would change everything. It wasn't easy. It required facing the lies I had believed about myself, replacing them with the truth of God's Word, and trusting Him to reshape how I thought, how I acted, and how I saw myself.

The Power of Renewing Your Mind

Renewing your mind isn't something you do once and move on. It's a daily choice—a commitment to let God's truth shape your thinking. As you do, you start to see yourself, your circumstances, and even other people through His eyes. That shift changes everything.

There's a peace and purpose that comes when you finally let God define who you are and how you live. But let's be real—it's not always comfortable. Letting go of old, ingrained beliefs that have shaped your life for years can feel like pulling up deep roots. Yet, as God's truth replaces those harmful thoughts, the freedom you gain is undeniable. Each step forward reveals a little more of who you really are in Christ: a beloved child with a unique purpose and a future full of hope.

Embracing the Journey

Transformation isn't a finish line you cross—it's a journey you walk. There will be moments on the mountaintop where everything feels clear and victorious, and there will be valleys where doubt and struggle try to hold you back. Both are part of the process.

Here are a few steps that can guide you along the way:

- **Reflect on What Needs to Change:** Be honest with yourself about what's holding you back.

- **Turn Struggles into Strength:** Trust that God can use even your most difficult moments to make you stronger.

- **Trade Fear for Faith:** Step forward in courage, knowing God's promises are bigger than your fears.

- **Let Pain Teach You:** Allow your past wounds to become a source of wisdom for the future.

- **See Setbacks as Stepping Stones:** View challenges as opportunities to grow closer to God and deepen your faith.

My Journey of Transformation

As I committed to renewing my mind, my life changed. The negative self-talk quieted, replaced by the truth of Scripture. I saw myself as God sees me—fearfully and wonderfully made, with a purpose only I could fulfill. That inner change didn't stop there. It spilled over into my relationships, my work, and even how I faced challenges. I began to see obstacles not as roadblocks, but as opportunities to lean on God's strength.

Most importantly, I learned to rely on the Holy Spirit. He became my guide, my comfort, and my source of power for true transformation. With each day, I grew more attuned to His voice, finding peace and direction in His leading.

The Holy Spirit: The Key to True Transformation

It's difficult to put in words the profound power and essential role of the Holy Spirit in my transformation—or in the journey of any believer. That's why the Holy Spirit will be a recurring theme throughout this book. Without Him, true transformation simply isn't possible.

Consider Zerubbabel's story. He was tasked with the overwhelming job of rebuilding the Temple's foundation and completing its construction, all while facing opposition and a lack of resources. Yet, God gave him this powerful assurance: "Not by might, nor by power, but by My Spirit." (Zechariah 4:6) This promise reminded Zerubbabel that human effort alone could never accomplish the task. It would take the power of God's Spirit to remove obstacles, leveling them as effortlessly as a tool smooths a mountain.

The same principle applies to our lives and the transformation God desires in us. Just as the Temple was the dwelling place of God among His people, believers are now His Temple, with the Holy Spirit living within us (1 Corinthians 6:19). Spiritual growth, character refinement, and breaking free from sin are no small feats. While discipline and determination are important, they can only take us so far. True change comes through the power of the Holy Spirit, working in and through us to achieve what we could never accomplish on our own.

The struggles we face—fear, bad habits, past hurts, or doubt—can feel like mountains that won't move. If we try to tackle them with just our own strength, they stay right where they are. But the steady and powerful work of the Holy Spirit can overcome even the toughest internal battles. He gives us the strength, wisdom, and grace to conquer what once seemed impossible.

When the prophet speaks of turning a great mountain into a flat plain, it symbolizes that every obstacle will be overcome—not by human effort, but through the Spirit's guidance and help. Glory to God!

The Power of the Spirit to Transform

The promise God gave Zerubbabel is the same for us today. Becoming more like Christ—showing the fruit of the Spirit, renewing our minds, and living faithfully—isn't something we can achieve just by trying harder. It's God's Spirit working in us, changing our desires, thoughts, and emotions. His power doesn't just make us better versions of ourselves; it makes us completely new in Christ:

"If anyone is in Christ, he is a new creation; old things have passed away; behold, all things have become new" (2 Corinthians 5:17). True transformation happens through the power of the Holy Spirit, who works in ways far beyond what we could ever do on our own.

Listen, it is through the power of the Holy Spirit that God equips us for the life He has called us to live—a life marked by grace, victory, and divine purpose. Just as Zechariah's prophecy assured Zerubbabel that the mountain before him would be leveled by God's Spirit, not human effort, we, too, can trust that our transformation will be accomplished by the Spirit of God working within us.

Transformation begins with understanding change. What is change, really? Is it simply altering our habits, or is it something deeper—a shift in our very being?

In the upcoming chapter, we will explore what change truly means and how embracing it opens the door to God's work in our lives.

CHAPTER 2

WHAT IS CHANGE?

C hange is the process of making or becoming something different. It's simple to define, but it can feel anything but simple. For some people, change brings excitement—like a new beginning filled with possibilities. For others, it creates fear and uncertainty—like facing a steep mountain.

But here's the truth: change is inevitable. It is part of life. Seasons shift, relationships grow or fade, and challenges arise, forcing us to adapt. If it's so natural, why does it feel overwhelming? Often it's because change can be intentional—something we plan—or unintentional; something that just happens.

Plan Change-Intentional

Intentional change starts with a decision. You choose a new direction—maybe breaking a harmful habit, choosing a new career, improving your health, or getting closer to God. This kind of change feels empowering because you're in control.

But even with the best intentions, the road is rarely easy. It demands courage, patience, and faith. You'll face obstacles that make you question whether it's worth it. Yet, when you keep your eyes on the goal, trusting

God to guide you, every step brings you closer to the life He's called you to live.

Unplanned Change—Unintentional

Unintentional. change often takes us by surprise—like a job loss, a health crisis, or a broken relationship. These moments can feel overwhelming because we didn't choose them. Yet they can also be the times when God works most deeply in our hearts. When life feels uncertain, His grace carries us. These painful seasons shape us in ways we might never have chosen but truly need, teaching us to trust God more and discover strengths we never knew we had.

Change; A Journey Worth Taking.

Change isn't easy, but it's worth it. Along the way, you'll face procrastination, self-doubt, and fear of failure. But with God's Word renewing your mind, the Holy Spirit guiding your steps, and His presence empowering you, no challenge is too great.

Transformation isn't just about what you do; it's about who you're becoming. It's about letting God reshape your heart and mind, aligning your life with His purpose. This journey is a partnership with the Creator, who has something extraordinary planned for you.

Understanding Change

Think of change as a journey. Like any trip, it takes time and happens in phases—recognizing the need for change, preparing for it, and then stepping forward. Ecclesiastes 3:1 reminds us, *"To everything, there is a season, and a time for every matter under heaven."* When we see change as a natural part of life, we can embrace it rather than resist it.

Change Through the Power of Faith

Change can be scary, but as believers, we're called to see it differently—as an opportunity to grow closer to God. Proverbs 3:5-6 encourages us: "Trust in the Lord with all your heart, and do not rely on your own understanding. In all your ways acknowledge Him, and He will make your paths straight."

Even when life feels uncertain, we can trust God is in control. Letting go of what we know and embracing the unknown isn't easy, but when we share our fears with Him, He fills us with peace and confidence for what's ahead.

Throughout this book, we will explore Biblical examples of transformative change that can completely alter a person's life. The apostle Paul's life serves as a powerful illustration of this transformation.

Biblical Examples of Change

The Bible is filled with stories of transformation. Saul of Tarsus—later known as the apostle Paul—experienced a profound change after encountering Jesus (Acts 9). Though his life took a dramatic turn, his growth continued beyond that initial experience. He wrestled with his humanity, yet he strove to live wholeheartedly for Christ.

Once a fierce opponent of the church, Paul found redemption in Jesus and was transformed. He let go of his old ways, even when the road ahead was daunting. His faith gave him the courage to embrace change, and it offers the same promise of transformation to each of us.

Transformation is a process. As Paul reminds us in Philippians 1:6 (AMP): *"He who has begun a good work in you will [continue to] perfect and complete it until the day of Christ Jesus [the time of His return]."* God doesn't expect instant perfection, but He does call us to keep growing.

Mental and Emotional Growth

The way we think and feel influences everything—how we see ourselves, how we connect with others, and how we move through life's challenges. Our emotions and beliefs create the lens through which we experience the world, shaping our well-being and how we approach every situation. It's a reminder of how powerful our mindset really is!

Emotional growth isn't easy, but it's so worth it. It's about facing those old wounds, letting go of beliefs that hold you back, and breaking free from negative thinking. It takes courage because it means dealing with parts of yourself you might have tried to ignore. But here's the thing—real transformation happens when you allow yourself to be vulnerable and do the hard work.

The Role of the Holy Spirit

The Holy Spirit plays a vital role in our journey of transformation. He guides us, empowers us, and shapes us to reflect the character of Christ. True and lasting change happens when we recognize His work in our lives and choose to surrender to it.

The discussion of the Holy Spirit's role will include more on this.

Each of these roles highlights the Holy Spirit's vital presence in a believer's life—offering guidance, strength, transformation, intercession, and comfort at every stage of the journey.

When we yield to the Holy Spirit's work, we experience profound and lasting change, drawing closer to Christ and living out our God-given purpose.

Physical Health: Caring for Your Body

Our bodies are sacred temples of the Holy Spirit (1 Corinthians 6:19), a priceless gift from our Heavenly Father. Taking care of them is a way to honor God and deepen our connection with Him. When we prioritize our physical health and fitness, we nurture not only our bodies but also our spiritual well-being. This allows us to serve God with more energy, face life's challenges with strength, and adapt more readily to His purpose for us.

Improving our nutrition and overall health is a vital part of this journey. Take a moment to pray and reflect: Are there habits that need to change? Weaknesses that need addressing? With God's guidance, we can identify these areas and start making positive changes.

It won't always be easy. Temptations and distractions will try to pull us off course. But with the Holy Spirit's guidance, along with faith and discipline, we can experience the transformation God desires for us.

Now, imagine the empowerment you'll feel as your health improves, your energy increases, and your outlook brightens. This renewed vitality doesn't just benefit you—it equips you to serve the Lord more effectively and deepens your confidence in His love. By caring for your body, you become a living testimony of how drawing closer to God transforms every aspect of life.

Let's commit to this journey of Christian self-improvement together. Trust that the Lord is with us every step of the way, and with His grace, there's nothing we can't achieve!

Healthy Relationships

Let's talk about relationships. Whether it's with family, friends, or your community, the people in your inner circle play a huge role in your happiness and growth. But let's be honest—relationships can get messy. Poor communication, weak boundaries, and unresolved conflicts can make things challenging.

What if it didn't have to stay that way? Healthy relationships start with strong communication—taking the time to really listen, being honest about your feelings, and showing empathy. It also means setting boundaries that protect your time, energy, and emotional well-being. When both people feel heard, valued, and respected, relationships flourish.

Sure, it takes effort. Healthy relationships don't just happen overnight. But when you put in the time and care, the rewards are worth it. You'll build stronger connections that bring more joy and meaning to your life. Start small—have that honest conversation you've been avoiding, or go out of your way to show someone how much you appreciate them. You'll be surprised at how much of a difference even small changes can make.

Change: Revamping Your Career and Financial Journey

How's work/business going? And how about your finances? These two areas can be significant sources of stress—or opportunities for growth. Whether you want to explore an alternative career path, learn a skill, or get your budget in order, the key is to take small, intentional steps.

If you're looking to grow in your career, maybe it's time to take on a new challenge or pursue some training to sharpen your skills. Or, if finances are the focus, start by figuring out where your money is going. Are there areas where you can cut back or save more? It may not seem like much, but even small changes can lead to significant results.

The important thing is to align your work and finances with your values. When you do, you'll find more satisfaction and purpose in both. Remember, progress is a process—celebrate each step forward.

Change: Financial Planning

Let's get real about money. It can feel overwhelming sometimes, right? But the truth is, getting a handle on your finances can bring so much freedom and peace. It's not about being perfect; it's about being intentional.

Start by asking yourself some honest questions. How are you earning, spending, and saving? Are there areas you want to improve? Yes, it can be uncomfortable to face these things, but taking that first step can lead to big changes. Maybe it's creating a budget, saving for something important, or just cutting back on unnecessary expenses.

Even small shifts can make a huge difference. Imagine the relief of knowing you're in control of your finances. You'll feel less stressed and more focused on what really matters. And the best part? Each step brings you closer to the life you want.

Conclusion

As we wrap up our discussion on **"What is Change,"** it's clear that change isn't a onetime event—it's a journey. It begins with awareness and unfolds through intentional steps, shaping us along the way. Together, we've explored what change truly is, why it's important, and how it impacts our lives.

Earlier, we explored the ideas of intended and unintended changes. One powerful example of unintended change is what I call "The Forged." This is the transformative process where God takes the painful experiences, injustices, and deep losses in our lives and repurposes them. Through His divine plan, He uses these trials to shape, refine, and prepare us for His purpose and our ultimate destiny.

When we begin to understand how God works through these moments, we experience a powerful shift in perspective. Instead of resisting, we learn to embrace the changes we once avoided, trusting that His hand is at work in every situation—turning trials into tools for good and growth.

Now get ready for to gain a new perspective, perhaps about a struggle you are dealing with now as we step into "The Forge."

CHAPTER 3

THE FORGED: THE FORCES OF CHANGE

In the previous chapter, we discussed the difference between **intentional** and **unintentional changes.** We will now add a third type of change to the mix: **The Forge—The Force of Change.**

Imagine a forge—a place of intense heat and relentless hammering where raw materials are transformed into tools of strength and purpose. It's a striking metaphor for the force of change in our lives. Just as a blacksmith uses fire and anvil to mold unyielding metal, so too does life's crucible shape us, through both intentional decisions and unforeseen trials.

Intentional change is like willingly stepping into the forge. It's the deliberate decision to embrace transformation, knowing it will require effort, surrender, and resilience. The process can be grueling—demanding courage, patience, and faith to endure the discomfort and uncertainty that growth often brings.

Unintentional change, on the other hand, feels like being thrust into the fire against your will. The flames of unexpected challenges and the blows of unanticipated setbacks test us in ways we never imagined. In those moments, it may seem like life is breaking us. Yet, these fiery trials are often where God's hand is most evident, purifying and reshaping us into something stronger, more beautiful, and perfectly aligned with His purpose.

In both cases, the forge represents the transformational power of surrendering to God's process.

The question isn't whether change will come—it will. The question is how we will respond. Will we resist, prolonging the pain, or will we trust the Master Craftsman, yielding to His design?

Lessons From The Life Of Joseph

Joseph's story is a testament to the power of God's refining process. When his own brothers, driven by jealousy, sold him into slavery, it must have felt like an unspeakable wound—an utter rejection by those he loved and trusted most. Yet, even during this painful heartbreak, God was quietly at work.

As a servant in Potiphar's household, Joseph distinguished himself through integrity, diligence, and a spirit of excellence. He could have become mired in self-pity, anger, or bitterness toward his brothers and even toward God. Instead, he flourished where he had was planted. Through faithfulness and perseverance, Joseph rose to a position of responsibility in Potiphar's household, mastering resource management, navigating relationships, and exercising leadership—skills he would one day apply on a grander scale.

This time of servitude was not wasted. Although it appeared to be a setback, it was, in truth, a divine assignment. God was equipping Joseph with discipline, humility, and the ability to steward whatever was entrusted to him. What seemed like a demotion was a season of preparation, laying the groundwork for the vital role he would later play.

Leadership Lessons in Prison

Just as Joseph began to find stability in Potiphar's house, he was falsely accused of a crime he did not commit and flung into prison. The injustice must have felt crushing. Yet, even in that dim, oppressive cell, the hand of God rested upon him. Prison became Joseph's unexpected training ground. There, amid people who had fallen from positions of influence, Joseph was placed in charge of managing the prison itself and caring for the inmates. It was here he honed his capacity to lead with compassion.

In this season, surrounded by those at their lowest point, he learned to guide and console the broken, to offer hope and maintain order in chaos. These lessons in human nature, character, and discernment would prove invaluable.

During this period of confinement, Joseph's God-given gift for interpreting dreams also came to light. His encounters with Pharaoh's cupbearer and baker were not mere coincidences; they were divine appointments that would ultimately lead to his release and ascent to power. The prison, though confining and uncomfortable, was an integral step in Joseph's preparation. By enduring hardship with grace and dependence on God, he emerged better equipped for the next phase of his journey.

The Widow and Her Jars: Uncovering Hidden Potential

Joseph's story is not the only biblical account showing how God uses forced change to uncover hidden potential. Consider the widow who turned to the prophet Elisha for help (2 Kings 4:1–7). Following her husband's death, she found herself overwhelmed by debt and faced the frightening prospect of losing her two sons to creditors. Destitute and desperate, she had no idea what to do next.

Desperate, she cried out to Elisha, who asked a simple yet profound question: 'What do you have in your house?' Her initial response reflected a scarcity mindset: 'Your servant has nothing there at all, except a small jar of olive oil.' (2 Kings 4:2, NIV).

Like many of us, she focused on what she lacked rather than what she had. But God frequently begins a transformation using what little we already have.

Elisha instructed her to borrow empty jars from her neighbors and begin pouring oil into them. It must have sounded strange. Still, in obedient faith, she followed his instructions. As she poured, the oil kept flowing until every borrowed jar was full. She sold the oil, paid off her debts, and still had enough to live on.

This widow—who likely never considered herself an entrepreneur—suddenly found herself running a small business. The forced change in her life, the death of her husband, had pushed her into a position where she discovered abilities and resourcefulness she never knew she had. Her story, like Joseph's, reminds us that God often uses our darkest moments to awaken potential and set us on new paths we never would have considered otherwise.

Embracing The Refining Process

Both Joseph and the widow illustrate a powerful truth: God often uses external circumstances to reveal the gifts and abilities He has placed within us. Being forced to adapt to change can deepen our reliance and trust in God, taking us beyond our comfort zone.

Joseph learned leadership through service, while the widow discovered entrepreneurial skills through faith. Both found purpose in hardship.

Undervaluing What We Have

How often do we, like the widow with her small jar of oil, fail to recognize the talents and resources God has placed in our hands? Could it be that you are undervaluing the very gifts, opportunities, and resources God has strategically provided for the challenge you are facing? Forced change has a remarkable way of shifting our perspective, revealing potential in what we might have overlooked or taken for granted.

Enduring Hardship

Change is rarely comfortable, especially when it arrives without an invitation. Our natural impulse is often to resist—clinging tightly to what we know, even if it no longer benefits us. But Joseph and the widow teach us that surrendering to God's process can turn trials into triumphs. Focusing on God and His promises helps us overcome hardship.

Redefining The Moment

Joseph refused to waste his servitude or prison years lamenting his plight or doubting God's plan. Instead, he embraced each season with hope and faithfulness, trusting there was purpose in his pain. Likewise, the widow did not dismiss Elisha's instructions as foolish. She acted in faith, even when the outcome seemed uncertain. By yielding to God's direction, both saw His faithfulness and power firsthand.

When we face unfair treatment, false accusations, health challenges, the loss of a relationship or marriage, financial difficulties, or business failure, we often find ourselves tested in ways that reveal our resilience and character. Yet, like Joseph, if we remain faithful to God and His Word, we can redefine 'the moment' by shifting our perspective to believe that what is happening to us is, in fact, working for us. This shift empowers us to confront obstacles with unwavering faith and a spirit of joy.

Romans 8:28 encourages us with the promise that God works all things together for the good of those who love Him and are called according to His purpose. This does not mean every situation will feel pleasant. It means that God can weave every hardship into His redemptive tapestry, using what was meant for harm to shape us, refine us, and lead us into something greater.

Both Joseph and the widow show us that change, though uncomfortable, is a tool in God's hands to reveal the gifts and abilities He has placed within us. There are four key object lessons we can learn from their example; we need to:

- **Recognize the Training Ground**: Every season has lessons to teach. Whether you're managing a home, enduring a challenging job, or walking through personal loss, ask God what He is shaping in you.

- **Look for What You Have**: It's easy to focus on what you lack, but God often begins with what's already in your hands. Seek His perspective to see hidden potential.

- **Step Out in Faith**: Both Joseph and the widow acted despite uncertainty. Faith requires obedience, even when the outcome isn't clear.

- **Trust God's Timing**: Joseph endured years of waiting, while the widow had to act swiftly. In both cases, God's timing was perfect.

Change rarely aligns with our preferred schedule. Joseph waited years for his dreams to be fulfilled, while the widow had to act swiftly to save her family. In both cases, God's timing was perfect. Trust that He is never early, never late, and always working behind the scenes for your good and His glory.

This Leads Us to Our Next Subject of Discussion: The Four Pillars of Change. As You Will See, Learning These Pillars Is a Must for Understanding Why We Seek Change.

CHAPTER 4

THE FOUR PILLARS OF CHANGE

Have you ever noticed that it's often at our lowest point that we finally become ready to change? Pain—whether it's physical, our emotions, or our spirit—shapes our journey with God in powerful ways.

While none of us enjoys going through hard times, these struggles often become exactly what we need to grow and find a deeper purpose.

Understanding How People Change

Renowned author John C. Maxwell identifies four elements that drive personal change. I have revised his four elements, which I call The Four Pillars of Change. These pillars represent the triggers that set the stage for sustainable growth and lasting impact:

We Change When Pain Pushes Us to Change

People change when they hurt enough that they have to. Pain often forces us out of our comfort zones. It might be losing someone we love, failing at something important, or facing a health crisis. During these hard times, many of us find the push we need to heal and grow. We see this in the Bible with Jonah—it took being in a fish's belly for him to finally obey God's call.

Inspired by Vision: Igniting the Flame of Change

People change when they see something that truly inspires them. A powerful vision can wake up dreams we've kept hidden. Sometimes, watching someone else's life change or suddenly understanding God's purpose can move us to action.

Look at Zerubbabel in the Bible—his vision to rebuild Jerusalem's temple didn't just excite him; it moved others to join him with focus and determination.

Receive The Knowledge They Need To Change

People change when they learn enough to want to. Knowledge is more than just gathering information—it's about gaining a deep understanding that reshapes how we see the world and how we live. Proverbs 4:7 reminds us, "The beginning of wisdom is this: Get wisdom. Though it cost all you have, get understanding." Pursuing wisdom equips us to make choices that align with God's plan for our lives.

Knowledge also sharpens our vision. Understanding God's Word can illuminate the path He has for us. However, gaining knowledge isn't always easy. It can lead to information overload or leave us feeling unsure of what to do next.

That's why it's so important to pray for discernment and seek wise counsel, ensuring that what we learn is applied in meaningful, God-honoring ways.

Provided Necessary Resources For Change

People change when they're given enough to make it possible. Sometimes what keeps us stuck isn't that we don't want to change—it's that we don't have the emotional support, spiritual guidance, or practical help we need. With God's power and the right resources, real change becomes possible.

Pain, The Number One Motivator For Change

When the pain of staying the same outweighs the pain of change, embracing a new path becomes preferable. Isn't it interesting how God often uses our struggles to guide us toward something better? It was "pain" that made me realize I needed to change. Otherwise, I would likely have continued with the status quo, hoping that things would one day get better.

Think about it—when was the last time you made a significant change in your life? Chances are, it occurred during a season of discomfort or challenges.

Let's be honest: none of us seeks pain. It tests our faith, stretches our endurance, and can lead us to question everything we once held dear. Yet, while God does not inflict pain upon us, He can use it as a means of growth and transformation. When life flows smoothly, we rarely feel the urgency to seek God's guidance or alter our course. But in our suffering, we often become more receptive to His gentle nudges toward a different path.

In my forty-plus years as a minister, counselor, and parent, I've seen this pattern repeatedly. Pain, more than any other force, lights a fire under us, compelling us to seek change. For some, the response may be a temporary fix—a band-aid to ease immediate hurt. For many, however, it is the first step on a journey toward a richer, more purposeful life aligned with God's will.

Have you ever stuck with a job, relationship, or habit, even after realizing it was wrong for you? The pain of staying stuck can become unbearable, can't it? Change becomes the better option when its discomfort is less than the suffering of staying put.

Sometimes, it is the very pain of change we try to avoid that God uses to shape us into who He is calling us to be. Or, to draw us to Him from the life that we live, that is not what He has purposed for us.

I'd like to tell you about a woman I counseled forty years ago. Let's call her Earline. Her story is a testament to how pain can serve to draw us to God and to He has purposed for us.

Earline's Story: From Pain to Redemption

The room was silent except for the faint hum of a clock ticking on the wall. Earline sat in the dim glow of a single lamp, her hands trembling as she clutched a worn photograph. It was a picture of her younger self, smiling brightly, unaware of the trials that lay ahead. How had she become so far removed from that girl—so beaten down by life? Another failed relationship, another crushing blow to her self-worth, another sleepless night wrestling with regret. Earline felt like a shipwreck in an endless storm, pieces of her scattered in the waves of heartbreak and failure.

She let the photograph fall onto the table and buried her face in her hands. "Do You even care, God?" Earline whispered, her voice barely audible. It wasn't the first time she had asked, but it felt like the first time she truly meant it. The silence that followed was deafening, as if even heaven had turned its back.

Days turned into weeks, and weeks into months. Earline went about her routine like a ghost, alive but not living. Her faith, once a flame that burned brightly, had long been reduced to cold ashes. Yet, even in her despair, she couldn't ignore the persistent whisper in her soul: *Keep going.*

At first, she dismissed it as wishful thinking. But the whisper grew louder, more insistent, until one Sunday morning, it compelled Earline to step out of her comfort zone and into unfamiliar territory—a church she had passed countless times but never entered. The very thought filled her with dread. What would they think of her? Could she ever feel as if she belong again after wandering so far?

The sanctuary buzzed with the warmth of greetings and laughter as Earline slipped into a back pew, hoping to remain unnoticed. But the moment she crossed the threshold, an inexplicable sense of peace washed over her. It was as if the walls themselves echoed with God's voice, saying, *Welcome home.*

As the service began, Earline sat stiffly, her hands clenched in her lap. The pastor's words were a balm and a blade, comforting her pain while slicing through the layers of denial she had built around her heart. He spoke of God's unwavering love and His relentless pursuit of the lost. "No matter how far you've strayed," he said, his voice steady and certain, "God is waiting to welcome you back."

Earline's chest tightened. Tears threatened to spill, but she blinked them away, unwilling to be vulnerable. Yet, the pastor's next words undid her completely: "There is no failure too great, no sin too deep, that can separate you from the love of God. He sees you. He knows your pain. And He is calling you."

It felt as if he were speaking directly to her, peeling back the layers of her soul to expose the raw, unspoken truths she had buried. A slideshow of her past flashed before her eyes—the betrayals, the mistakes, the nights she had cried herself to sleep. Earline wanted to run, but her feet felt rooted to the floor.

When the pastor invited those seeking a fresh start to come forward, Earline froze. Fear gripped her like a vise. The voice of condemnation whispered harshly in her ear, *You're not good enough. You've failed too many times. God won't take you back.*

But then, piercing through the noise, she heard another voice—a quiet, tender whisper: *Do you trust Me?*

It was the same voice that had urged her to keep going. Earline's heart raced as she clung to the words, letting them drown out the lies. *Do you trust Me?* The question echoed in her spirit, filling her with a courage she hadn't felt in years.

Her hands moved to her chest, as if to shield her breaking heart. "Yes, God," she whispered, her voice trembling. "I trust You."

In that moment, something shifted. The weight Earline had carried for so long began to lift, replaced by a warmth that felt like sunlight breaking through the darkest storm clouds. Tears spilled freely as she rose from her seat, her steps unsteady but determined. Each step toward the altar felt like shedding another chain, another layer of shame and regret.

Kneeling at the altar, Earline wept openly, pouring out her heart in a prayer of repentance and surrender. The words tumbled out in a rush—words she hadn't spoken aloud in years. As she confessed her failures and fears, Earline felt an overwhelming sense of release, as if God Himself were gently gathering the shattered pieces of her heart and making them whole again.

For the first time in what felt like forever, she felt seen. Loved. Redeemed. It wasn't just the pastor's words or the warmth of the congregation that had brought her to this moment—it was the undeniable presence of God, wrapping her in an embrace that whispered, *You are Mine.*

When Earline finally stood, her face was streaked with tears, but her heart was lighter than it had been in years. Earline didn't know what the future held, but she knew one thing for certain: she was no longer walking it alone. God had called her back, and she had answered.

The Four Pillars Impact on Earline

Earline's story exemplifies the Four Pillars of change. Her pain pushed her to seek help. The vision of a restored relationship with God inspired hope. The knowledge she gained from the pastor's sermon helped her make a decision to come back to God. And the support from Earline's church community provided the necessary resources for lasting transformation.

Pain: The Catalyst for Change and Renewal

Pain commands our attention, forcing us to reflect on our lives. Earline's pain motivated her to seek change. When we are comfortable, it's easy to become complacent and settle into unhealthy routines. Hardship, however, wakes us up.

Pain often serves as a wake-up call, prompting us to make changes we might have otherwise resisted or ignored. During these challenging times, we gain a fresh perspective on our priorities and find the motivation to act.

Earline's journey vividly demonstrates the transformative power of pain. Faced with a choice—endure her suffering or open herself to God's transforming work—she chose faith. In response, God met her with love, healing, and the purpose she desperately needed.

Now, take a moment to reflect: Where are you on your journey? Are you feeling lost, as Earline once did, searching for a way forward? Or are you already taking steps toward the life God is calling you to?

When was the last time you learned something so profound it changed how you think or act? Could it be that seeking God's wisdom is the key to the change you're longing for?

This idea of pain driving transformation isn't new. Jesus beautifully illustrates it in the Parable of the Prodigal Son, a story that highlights how pain and brokenness can ignite a journey back to God and the life we're meant to live. Let's dive into this parable to see how even the deepest struggles can become a turning point for transformation.

The Story of the Prodigal Son

Jesus tells of a father with two sons. The younger son, impatient for independence, demands his inheritance early. With his newfound wealth, he leaves home and squanders it in reckless living. Eventually, he hits rock bottom, penniless and alone in a distant land.

Let's follow his story or redemption, "The Awakening"

The sun blazed mercilessly over the barren road as the young man trudged onward, his tattered clothes clinging to his weary frame. Dust clung to his bare feet, the sandals long gone—sold days ago for a meager meal. His stomach ached with the relentless gnaw of hunger. Three days without food, a cruel testament to just how far he had fallen.

His thoughts swirled like a storm, memories of feasts and laughter at his father's table mocking his current state. How could he have been so reckless, so blind?

Once, he had stood proud and bold, demanding his share of the inheritance. His father's eyes had been full of sorrow, not anger, as he divided his wealth. The younger son didn't care—freedom was his, and with a heavy purse, he set out for a distant land. Life became a blur of indulgence: endless parties, shallow companions, and a reckless pursuit of pleasure. But like a flame burning too brightly, it soon consumed everything.

When the famine struck, it didn't just steal the land's harvest—it stole his illusions. Penniless and abandoned, he found himself feeding pigs, the lowest of the low, his stomach twisting as he envied their slop. It was there, in the filth of that pigpen, that clarity pierced his despair. He remembered his father's servants—how even they had food to spare. Shame flooded him, but with it came resolve. *I will go home,* he thought. *I'll tell my father I'm no longer worthy to be his son. Perhaps he will hire me as a servant.*

The journey home felt endless, each step a battle against fear. What if his father turned him away? What if he had burned that bridge forever? But as he neared the familiar horizon, something incredible happened.

Far off, silhouetted against the golden glow of the setting sun, was a figure. His father. The old man's gait was hurried, almost stumbling, as he ran to meet his son. The younger man froze, overwhelmed by a mix of dread and longing. Before he could speak, his father's arms enveloped him, the embrace warm and unyielding.

"Father," the son choked, tears spilling down his dirt-streaked cheeks. "I have sinned against heaven and against you. I'm no longer worthy to be called your son."

But his father didn't listen to the rehearsed apology. He stepped back, his face radiant with joy. "Quick!" he called to the servants who had followed. "Bring the finest robe and put it on him! Place a ring on his finger and sandals on his feet. Prepare a feast, for this son of mine was dead and is alive again; he was lost and is found!"

As the servants hurried to obey, the son stood stunned. He had expected rejection, at best tolerance. But instead, he found restoration. The robe symbolized honor, the ring of authority, and the family's specially crafted sandals all were symbolic of sonship. His father wasn't just welcoming him back; he was restoring him as a son.

Jesus told this parable to paint a picture of God's love—a love that sees us at our worst and still runs to meet us. The father's embrace mirrors the embrace of our Heavenly Father, whose mercy knows no bounds. No sin is too great, no distance too far, to separate us from His love.

In life, like the prodigal son, we may stray. We may find ourselves in a place of emptiness, facing the consequences of our choices. Yet, it's often in these moments of desperation that we hear God's call to return. It's not a call of condemnation but of compassion, an invitation to repentance and restoration.

This parable reminds us that God doesn't merely tolerate our return—He celebrates it. The feast isn't just a meal; it's a declaration of His joy over every soul that comes back to Him.

Through the prodigal son's story, Jesus offers a profound truth: redemption is always within reach. No matter how far we've fallen, God's arms remain open, ready to welcome us home. Our hardships, like the son's time in the pigpen, can become the turning point, "The Awakening" that leads us back to Him. It is in His embrace that we find healing, belonging, and the hope of a new beginning.

Awareness of the Need to Change

Luke 15:17–18 captures a life-changing moment: "But when he came to himself, he said, 'How many of my father's hired servants have bread enough and to spare, and I perish with hunger! I will arise and go to my father and say to him, 'Father, I have sinned against heaven and before you...'"

Awareness is always the first step toward meaningful change. When Jesus says the son "came to himself," He highlights the power of self-awareness—recognizing the reality of our situation. This involves understanding where we are, imagining where we need to be, and identifying the steps to bridge that gap. Without this awakening, transformation remains out of reach.

(I'll delve deeper into the concept of 'Awareness' in a future discussion.)

For the prodigal son, it was his hunger and desperation that pushed him to confront the mistakes he'd made and the life he had lost. He realized how much he longed for his father's love, the security he'd abandoned, and the home he had taken for granted. Even though he knew returning would mean facing shame and humility, he understood it was the only way forward.

This moment of clarity sets the stage for the next essential step—deciding to act. It's one thing to recognize the need for change; it's another to embrace it and take action.

Deciding To Change

Choosing to change is just the first step—action has to follow. Real transformation starts with a decision, but without the commitment to follow through, that decision won't lead to lasting change. "A double-minded man is unstable in all his ways." (James 1:8)

The prodigal son's resolve to return home, and the steps he took, led him into his father's warm embrace. Here, he found comfort, restoration, and acceptance. His story perfectly illustrates the significance of self-awareness and purposeful action in reconnecting with our Heavenly Father.

When we face physical, emotional, or spiritual discomfort, it's natural to seek relief. The world offers countless temporary fixes—distractions, unhealthy habits, or quick solutions that promise comfort, but leave us feeling just as empty as before. These fleeting comforts may dull the pain for a moment, but they can never address the deeper issues in our hearts.

Closing Thoughts on the "Four Pillars of Change

In exploring the Four Pillars of Change—pain, vision, knowledge, and empowerment—we've uncovered the foundational elements that drive meaningful and lasting transformation. Pain serves as the catalyst, pushing us beyond our comfort zones; vision ignites our dreams and inspires action; knowledge equips us with the wisdom to navigate our journey; and empowerment provides the necessary resources and support to sustain our growth.

Earline's journey and the Prodigal Son's redemption illustrate how these pillars interconnect, guiding us through our darkest moments toward a place of healing and purpose. As you reflect on your own experiences, consider how these pillars can support your path to spiritual renewal. Embrace the pain as a stepping stone, seek a vision that aligns with God's purpose, pursue knowledge with a humble heart, and lean on the resources God provides.

Remember, transformation is not an overnight process but a journey of faith and perseverance. By grounding yourself in these principles, you can navigate life's challenges with resilience and grace, trusting that God is guiding you every step of the way.

Let these pillars be your guide as you step into the life God has prepared for you, marked by peace, purpose, and divine alignment.

Now that we have studied the definition and biblical concepts of change, it's time to define and understand "transformation," the true objective of change.

CHAPTER 5

UNDERSTANDING TRANSFORMATION

When you think of transformation, what image comes to mind? Picture an old, neglected house being renovated—workers carefully stripping away worn-out layers, repairing broken foundations, and creating a space that feels brand new.

Or imagine a chaotic, overgrown yard slowly being cleared, planted, and nurtured until it becomes a beautiful, thriving garden.

These transformations don't happen overnight; they require vision, patience, and dedicated effort. Now think about your own life—what would true transformation look like for you?

For Christians, transformation goes far deeper than external changes. Unlike renovating a house or tending a garden, spiritual transformation isn't just about fixing things on the outside or trying to be better through our own efforts.

It's an inside job—a profound process where God himself reshapes us to become more like Jesus. This transformation is not merely superficial; it goes deep into the core of our being, challenging us to confront our fears and insecurities. It's about letting go of old, broken patterns and allowing God's grace to create something entirely new and beautiful in us.

As we surrender to this divine process, we find ourselves shedding the weight of past mistakes and embracing a future filled with hope and purpose. In this journey, we learn that true change often requires patience and perseverance, but the rewards of a renewed spirit are immeasurable. Ultimately, this inner work enables us to reflect God's love and compassion in our daily lives, impacting those around us in profound ways.

Christian Transformation: Made New in Christ

The Apostle Paul captures this profound truth in 2 Corinthians 5:17 (NIV): "Therefore, if anyone is in Christ, the new creation has come: The old has gone, the new is here!"

Is there a moment in your life where you've felt the need for a fresh start, a new beginning? It's not about polishing up the surface or masking imperfections. It's about being completely remade by God. When you place your faith in Jesus, He doesn't just improve the old version of you—He makes you entirely new. Your past, your failures, your shortcomings—they no longer define you.

Isn't that an incredible thought? Through Christ, you are not bound by what you once were. God's transforming power is at work, shaping you into the person He created you to be.

The Elements of True Transformation

Just as a master builder follows a careful plan for renovation, God's transformation in our lives unfolds through specific elements that guide us toward lasting change. When we look to Scripture, we discover five key components that define biblical transformation—those pivotal moments and decisions that align us with God's purpose and reshape us from the inside out. Let's explore these essential elements together.

1. Spiritual Rebirth

Can you recall the joy of a fresh start? In Christ, we are given the ultimate new beginning—spiritual rebirth. Jesus explains this clearly in John 3:3 (NIV): "Very truly I tell you, no one can see the kingdom of God unless they are born again."

This rebirth is not about improving your behavior or turning over a new leaf. It's a complete renewal of your spirit, a miracle made possible through the Holy Spirit. Salvation marks the beginning of this journey. It's the moment when God breathes new life into you and sets you on a path toward Him.

Can you recall the moment you first encountered God's love? That overwhelming sense of peace and hope? That's where transformation begins—with Him.

2. Continuous Renewal

Think about how change often unfolds gradually, like a sunrise bringing light little by little. While salvation is immediate, transformation unfolds over time. Day by day, we are called to renew our minds and hearts, aligning ourselves more fully with God's will. The Apostle Paul urges us in Romans 12:2 (NIV): "Do not conform to the pattern of this world, but be transformed by the renewing of your mind."

As you spend time in God's Word and seek His guidance, your thoughts, attitudes, and actions begin to change. It's not about striving to be perfect; it's about allowing God to work in you, shaping your heart to reflect His love.

3. Holistic Change

What happens when a single change sets off a cascade of transformation in your life? True transformation with God touches every part of who you are:

Emotional Healing: He mends broken hearts and restores peace.

Mental Renewal: He replaces lies with His truth, giving clarity and wisdom.

Behavioral Growth: He empowers you to live in ways that honor Him.

Relational Restoration: He brings forgiveness and reconciliation into your relationships.

Spiritual Growth: He cultivates in you the fruit of the Spirit—love, joy, peace, and more.

Take a moment to reflect: Which area of your life needs God's transforming touch the most right now?

4. Divine Empowerment

Here's an encouraging truth: You don't have to walk this journey alone. Transformation is not about relying on your own strength; it's about trusting in God's power. Philippians 2:13 (NIV) reminds us: "For it is God who works in you to will and to act in order to fulfill his good purpose."

Do you find yourself striving to change, only to feel the weight of the effort on your own shoulders? God never intended for us to bear that weight. He works within us, giving us the strength and desire to grow. When you feel weak, lean into His power. He's there to carry you.

5. Purpose-Driven Transformation

Do you ever wonder why God is transforming you? It's not just for your benefit—it's so you can fulfill the unique calling He has for your life. As you're changed, you reflect God's glory to the world, becoming a beacon of hope and love. Your transformation isn't just about you; it's about impacting others for His kingdom.

How Do We Embrace This Transformation?

Transformation requires action, surrender, and trust. Here are ways to embrace the process:

Get into God's Word: Make time to study and meditate on Scripture. Let His truth renew your mind and guide your decisions each day. By immersing yourself in His teachings, you will find clarity and purpose that can influence every aspect of your life.

Pray Daily: Speak to God and listen for His voice. Prayer is where transformation begins, as it creates a pathway for spiritual growth and deeper connection. Remember that this dialogue is not just about speaking; it involves being still and receptive to the guidance and inspirations He offers.

Build Community: Surround yourself with believers who encourage and challenge you in your faith. Engaging with a supportive group can provide you with new perspectives and insights, helping you to grow in ways you may not have anticipated. These relationships can also foster accountability, prompting you to stay committed to personal and spiritual development.

Surrender Control: Trust God in every area of your life, even the ones you're afraid to let go of. Recognizing that His plan is greater than your own can free you from the burden of needing to manage every detail. This surrender is an act of faith that opens doors to a deeper relationship with Him.

Receive God's Love: Open your heart to the love of God, knowing it has the power to heal and restore. Allowing yourself to truly experience His love can instill a sense of belonging and security that transcends life's challenges. It is within this love that you can find your true identity and purpose.

As you take these steps, ask yourself: What is one small way I can invite God to transform me today? Consider setting intentions each morning that can help guide your actions, making the process of transformation a continual and intentional part of your daily life. Embracing these practices not only deepens your faith but also enriches the lives of those around you.

The Role of Repentance in Transformation

Before transformation begins, we must answer God's call to repentance. Repentance is not about guilt or shame—it's about turning away from sin and turning toward God. It's the moment we say, "Lord, I need You. Change me."

John the Baptist proclaimed in Matthew 3:2 (NIV): "Repent, for the kingdom of heaven has come near."

Repentance prepares our hearts for the work God wants to do in us. It's like clearing away the rubble so that God can build something new. Can you recall the freedom and peace that comes after bringing your burdens to God in repentance? That's the freedom repentance brings.

(There is an in-depth study of "The Role of Repentance" in chapter 21).

God's Promise For Your Transformation

Transformation is not just about the destination—it's about the journey, walking hand in hand with God as He makes all things new. Are you ready to let Him shape your life in ways you never imagined?

In the next chapter, we'll dive deeper into repentance and explore how a single encounter with Jesus, like Zacchaeus experienced, can turn everything around.

God's invitation to transformation is for you. Will you say yes?

CHAPTER 6

A PORTRAIT OF GRACE: A MAN NAMED ZACCHAEUS

Life can change in an instant. For some, transformation is a gradual process—a journey of small, steady steps over time. For others, it happens in a single, life-changing moment. Take Zacchaeus, for example. His entire life was turned around the day he met Jesus.

In Luke 19:1-10, the story of Zacchaeus paints a striking picture of grace in action. It shows how a true encounter with the Savior can lead to immediate and lasting change. His transformation is a powerful testament to the impact of repentance and the incredible work Jesus can do in a willing heart.

Zacchaeus's change wasn't just deep—it was instant. His story reminds us that when we come to Jesus with open hearts, our lives are never the same.

The Man Behind The Story

Zacchaeus was a tax collector, and not just any tax collector—he was the chief tax collector in the city of Jericho. In the eyes of his fellow Jews, this position placed him among the most despised in society. The occupying Roman government employed tax collectors, who enriched themselves at the expense of their own people. Zacchaeus was no exception. His wealth, likely amassed through dishonest practices, only deepened the disdain others felt toward him.

Though he rarely admitted it—even to himself—there were nights when Zacchaeus lay awake, haunted by the silent accusations of his conscience. The countless faces of those he had cheated and betrayed over the years flickered through his mind, as did the bitter knowledge that despite his fine clothes and grand home, he had no genuine friends.

The whispered insults from his neighbors, the pitying looks, the sidelong glances from strangers—all these cut him deeply, though he would never show it. He wore his wealth like a shield against the world's contempt, yet deep down he felt isolated, stained by his past choices and uncertain of his future. He wondered if there was any escape from the life he had chosen. Wealth could not buy him acceptance, peace, or a sense of purpose.

Zacchaeus encounter with Jesus would reveal a man ready for change, desperate for something more than the hollow life he had built for himself.

The Search for Jesus

Zacchaeus heard Jesus was passing through Jericho. Jesus, they said, was different. He spoke with authority, yet welcomed those that society despised—sinners, tax collectors, and the brokenhearted. Some even claimed He was the promised Messiah, the One long foretold, whose kingdom was near. Zacchaeus had heard John the Baptist's words echoing through the region: "Repent, for the kingdom of heaven has come near." He never thought those words could apply to someone like him. Yet something about Jesus compelled him to find out more.

But how could he? The streets were packed, and Zacchaeus, small in stature, stood no chance of seeing over the crowd. Determined and anxious, he dashed ahead and scrambled up a sycamore tree. Perched among the leaves, heart pounding, he could see the throng pressing around a Man at the center—Jesus. As he waited, an unexpected mixture of hope and dread churned in his stomach. Would this famed Teacher notice him at all? If He did, would He scorn him like everyone else, call him a sinner to his face, and expose his shame?

The Moment of Encounter

As Jesus approached, the crowd surged forward, jostling and clamoring for His attention. Suddenly, Jesus stopped. He looked up. For a moment, their eyes met—Zacchaeus, breathless and trembling among the branches, and Jesus, whose gaze was filled not with disgust or condemnation, but with compassion and understanding. Zacchaeus inhaled sharply. He felt seen—truly seen—for the first time in his life.

"Zacchaeus," Jesus called, voice carrying warmth and welcome, "come down immediately. I must stay at your house today." (Luke 19:5, NIV)

The invitation stunned him. The Teacher knew his name. He knew his name. How could that be? Why would Jesus—revered by so many—want to dine with a notorious tax collector like him? Zacchaeus' heart twisted with emotion. Here was a chance, a lifeline. With shaking limbs, he began climbing down, cheeks flushed, eyes shining with a mixture of gratitude and disbelief.

The crowd murmured in disbelief as Zacchaeus climbed down from the tree, his movements unsteady yet filled with urgency. Whispers spread like wildfire: *Why would Jesus, a holy teacher, associate with someone like him? A tax collector? A sinner?* The weight of their judgment pressed against Zacchaeus, but something far stronger—Jesus' unwavering invitation—drew him forward.

Zacchaeus, descending carefully from the lowest branch because of his small stature, landed just a few yards away from where Jesus stood. Heart pounding, he began walking toward the Lord, his steps deliberate despite the sneers and icy stares piercing through him like a winter's fog. Each judgmental glance weighed heavy, but Zacchaeus pressed on, drawn by something greater than the crowd's disdain.

At last, Zacchaeus stood before Jesus. In the eyes of the world, he felt small and unimportant, but in that moment, he knew he was fully seen and deeply valued by the One who called him by name.

For years, Zacchaeus had hidden behind his riches and power, using his position to protect himself from the rejection and judgment of others. Yet here was Jesus, looking at him not with condemnation, but with compassion—a look that seemed to say, *I see you, not as you are in the eyes of the world, but as you were created to be.* In that instant, something cracked open inside him—a barrier he had erected long ago to protect himself from pain and judgment.

For Zacchaeus, Jesus' recognition of him and His desire to spend time with him were like a key, unlocking the floodgates of remorse, longing, and desperate hope he had buried deep within his heart for so long. The two began walking together toward Zacchaeus' home, and the crowd's grumbles grew louder. "He has gone to be the guest of a sinner!" someone hissed.

The words stung, but for the first time, they didn't matter. Zacchaeus' gaze remained fixed on Jesus, who walked beside him as though the world's opinions held no power.

The Transformation Begins

Inside his home, as the meal was prepared and served, Zacchaeus' heart burned with an unfamiliar mix of joy and conviction. He couldn't stay silent any longer. Rising to his feet, he looked at Jesus with tears streaming down his face and declared, "Look, Lord! Here and now I give half of my possessions to the poor, and if I have cheated anybody out of anything, I will pay back four times the amount." (Luke 19:8, NIV)

Zacchaeus' words weren't planned or for show. They poured out from a heart completely overwhelmed by grace. He wasn't trying to earn Jesus' approval—he already had it. This was his response: a real act of repentance, turning from his old ways and stepping toward the person Jesus was calling him to become.

This was no small gesture. As a wealthy man, Zacchaeus' choice to give half of his possessions to the poor and repay those he had cheated went far beyond what Jewish law required. The law only asked for the original amount stolen plus one-fifth as a penalty (Leviticus 6:5). But Zacchaeus went further, showing just how deeply his heart had been changed.

His transformation was undeniable. After meeting Jesus, the riches Zacchaeus once clung to now seemed worthless compared to the treasure he found in the Messiah. He resolved to return what he had taken, right his wrongs, and start fresh. This was repentance in action—a changed heart revealed through his deeds.

The Response Of The Crowd

Not everyone was pleased with Jesus' decision to dine with Zacchaeus. The crowd muttered, disapproving. How could Jesus dine with a sinner like him? Yet Jesus looked beyond Zacchaeus' past and saw a man humbled, ready to embrace the kingdom of God.

Jesus' response to the crowd was simple yet profound: "Today salvation has come to this house, because this man, too, is a son of Abraham. For the Son of Man came to seek and to save the lost" (Luke 19:9-10, NIV).

In this declaration, Jesus affirmed Zacchaeus' place in the family of God and reminded everyone of His mission: to seek and save those who are lost.

Zacchaeus could hardly believe it. That very morning, he had awakened as an outcast—hated and despised by society, and outside the covenant of God. Yet now, he stood as a welcomed member of God's family. He was no longer defined by his past mistakes or his reputation in the eyes of others. He was seen, known, and loved by the Savior who had come to redeem even the most unlikely.

The Immediacy of Grace

Zacchaeus' story shows the power of grace to work instantly. His transformation didn't need a long process or a checklist of requirements. The moment he met Jesus, everything changed. This doesn't mean Zacchaeus didn't have other issues he would have to work through with the help of the Holy Spirit. However, the direction of his life was forever altered. His generosity and efforts to make things right were clear signs of the change that had taken place in his heart.

This immediacy of grace is available to us, too. When we encounter Jesus with open hearts, He meets us with forgiveness, acceptance, and love. We don't have to clean ourselves up or fix our lives before coming to Him. Zacchaeus didn't climb down from the tree with a plan to make amends. He simply responded to Jesus' invitation, and the transformation followed.

Lessons From Zaccheus' Transformation

Zacchaeus' story offers powerful lessons for anyone seeking transformation:

1. **Humility Prepares the Heart:** Zacchaeus humbled himself by climbing a tree, letting go of the pride and dignity tied to his status. Transformation starts when we recognize our need for Jesus and approach Him with a humble heart.

2. **Jesus Meets Us Where We Are:**
   Zacchaeus didn't have to go to the synagogue or follow a religious ritual to meet Jesus. Jesus came to him, saw him in his brokenness, and extended an invitation. No matter where you are in life, Jesus is ready to meet you.

3. **Grace Leads to Action:** True transformation is marked by action. Zacchaeus didn't just feel sorry for his wrongs—he acted on it. His generosity and efforts to make amends were proof of the change that had taken place in his heart.

4. **Transformation Is Immediate and Ongoing:** Zacchaeus' transformation happened in an instant, but it was just the start of a lifelong journey of growth and renewal.

Meeting Jesus puts us on a new path, but the journey of faith continues as we draw closer to Him and strive to reflect His character more each day.

This process requires intentionality and an ever-deepening awareness of His presence in our lives.

Conclusion

Zacchaeus' story is a powerful reminder that no one is beyond the reach of God's grace. Even with a past marked by greed and dishonesty, Zacchaeus wasn't excluded from a future with Jesus. What truly changed his life wasn't his position or his past—it was his desire to seek Jesus and his readiness to respond to His invitation.

If you've ever felt like Zacchaeus—lost in the crowd, burdened by guilt, or unsure where to turn—or if you've faced rejection, feeling unloved or unwanted, know this: Jesus is calling your name. He sees you, knows you, and desires to be with you. Just as Zacchaeus experienced, a single moment of surrender can open the door to God's transformative grace.

Zacchaeus was welcomed by Jesus without judgment, criticism, or rejection. The same grace and acceptance are available to you. Jesus is ready to meet you where you are, no matter your past or present. All He asks is that you believe in Him as your Savior, sent by God to pay the price for your sins and raised from the dead so you might have eternal life. Through repentance and faith, you can receive the gift of salvation and begin a new life in Him.

If you're ready to take this step, you can pray this simple prayer from your heart:

"Heavenly Father, I come to You in the name of Jesus. I confess that I am a sinner, and I seek Your forgiveness. I believe that Jesus Christ is Your Son, that He died for my sins, and that He rose from the dead. I ask You to forgive me of my sins and cleanse me. Today, I accept Jesus Christ as my Lord and Savior, and I surrender my life

to Him. Thank You for saving me and making me a part of Your family. In Jesus' name, Amen."

If you prayed that prayer sincerely, know this: You are now part of God's family! Jesus has drawn near to you, and your life is forever changed. Welcome to the family of God! Your journey with Him has just begun, and the transformation He brings will touch every part of your life.

I have a free eBook I'd love to share with you entitled *The Walk of Faith*. This book is designed to help you discover your new identity as a Christian and guide you on your journey as a Believer in Christ. Packed with practical insights and instructions, it provides the tools you need to navigate your new life of faith with confidence and purpose. Let this resource be a companion as you grow deeper in your walk with God.

To receive your free copy, simply email me at **faithclinic77@gmail.com** and request *The Walk of Faith* eBook. I'll send it to you at no cost. Start your journey of faith today.

Listen, just as Zacchaeus' life became a testimony to the immediacy and power of Jesus' love, so too can yours. Transformation may come in a moment, but its impact will last a lifetime. Step out, climb down, and welcome Jesus into your heart. The journey of a lifetime begins with a single step of faith.

Zacchaeus experienced a transformation that not only changed his mind, but also gave him a new heart. In the upcoming chapter, we will explore how this provision of a new heart is part of God's divine plan for all His children.

CHAPTER 7

A NEW HEART, A NEW YOU

Have you ever heard someone described as cold-hearted or hard-hearted? These words create a vivid image of someone lacking empathy, compassion, or warmth—a person distant, perhaps even indifferent to the struggles of those around them.

This was likely how people saw Zacchaeus. As a chief tax collector, he was despised for his greed and betrayal of his own people. Yet beneath his hardened exterior, something stirred—a longing that led him to a life-changing encounter with Jesus.

But let's turn that lens inward. Have you ever felt as though your own heart had grown cold? Maybe forgiving someone feels impossible, or showing love to those who frustrate you seems out of reach. Perhaps you've struggled to sense God's presence, feeling spiritually distant or weighed down by life's burdens.

At times, it may feel as though your heart has turned to stone—hardened by pain, disappointment, or sin. Yet even in that state, there is hope. God doesn't leave us in our brokenness. He offers an extraordinary promise to transform our hearts completely, replacing the cold and unresponsive with something tender, alive, and full of His love.

Are you ready to let Him begin that transformation in you?

The Promise

"A new heart also will I give you, and a new spirit will I put within you: and I will take away the stony heart out of your flesh, and I will give you an heart of flesh."

Background and Context:

Ezekiel 36 is a message of restoration and hope given to the people of Israel during their exile. They were scattered because of their disobedience to God, but He promises to bring them back—not only to their land, but into a renewed relationship with Him. Verse 26 speaks about a deep, inner transformation that God offers. It's a promise to change His people from the inside out so they can live in harmony with His will.

What Is A New Heart?

"A new heart also will I give you..."

What It Means: The "new heart" symbolizes a complete renewal of a person's inner self. In biblical terms, the heart represents emotions, thoughts, and decision-making. A "new heart" means a fresh ability to desire what is good and to love and follow God. God's Grace in Action: This promise shows that God's work in our lives is a gift, not something we can achieve on our own. He willingly replaces our old, sinful ways with something entirely new.

"...and a new spirit will I put within you:"

What It Means: The "new spirit" represents a renewed mindset or attitude. It aligns a person's thoughts and emotions with God's will, making them open and eager to follow Him. The Holy Spirit's Role: This promise points to the work of the Holy Spirit, who, after Christ's resurrection, comes to live within believers. The Spirit gives strength, guidance, and the ability to live a godly life.

"...and I will take away the stony heart out of your flesh..."

What It Means: A "stony heart" is a symbol of stubbornness, pride, and resistance to God. It describes a spiritual state where someone refuses to listen to or obey God. God Removes Obstacles: God promises to remove this hard, unresponsive heart, replacing it with something soft and alive, capable of change.

"...and I will give you an heart of flesh."

What It Means: A "heart of flesh" is soft, sensitive, and responsive to God. It symbolizes a person who is ready to follow His commands and live in a relationship with Him. Transformation: With this new heart, God's people will not only obey Him out of duty, but will love and trust Him deeply, living in harmony with His plans.

Key Lessons for Us Today

True Change Begins in the Heart: This verse reminds us that real transformation doesn't start with outward actions, but with a change of heart. God replaces the old, sinful ways with a new heart that desires to do what is right.

The Holy Spirit Brings Renewal: The "new spirit" points to the role of the Holy Spirit, who lives within believers today. The Spirit teaches us, gives us strength, and helps us grow closer to God.

Hope for Hardened Hearts: Even if someone feels distant from God or stuck in sin, this verse shows that God can change them. He takes hearts that are hardened and makes them soft and alive, able to respond to Him.

You might ask yourself, "If God has given me a new heart, why am I not seeing any difference?" That's a good question! The answer lies in understanding that God fulfills His promise of a new heart at the moment of our rebirth—when we are Born Again. However, it's crucial to recognize that while God gives us this gift, it is our responsibility to live from it. Transformation requires not just receiving the new heart but also aligning our thoughts, actions, and choices with it.

When we are born again, we are made new creations in Christ Jesus, becoming born-again spirits and children of God. God gifts us the Holy Spirit to guide us and gives us a new heart to facilitate our transformation. However, He does not change our minds, as they represent our free will — a precious gift from God. With our new heart, influenced and guided by the Holy Spirit, we are empowered to renew our minds by immersing ourselves in the Word of God (Romans 12:2).

Some believers might not fully experience the transformative power of their new heart because they often allow their old, un-renewed mind to guide them. Our new heart encourages us to pray, study the Word of God, and follow the guidance of the Holy Spirit. Conversely, our old mindset, influenced by the world around us, tends to seek a self-serving and misguided path, which hinders us from fully embracing the new spirit we have received.

Another important reason some believers find it difficult to live according to the new heart that God has granted them is that they are unaware of the God-given abilities they now have. By the power of the Holy Spirit and the Word of God, believers can transform and reprogram their minds to align with God's purpose for their lives. One aim of this book is to help believers increase their awareness.

The Divine Heart Transplant

"A new heart also will I give you, and a new spirit will I put within you..." This promise is a divine heart transplant. And here's the beautiful part: it's not something we have to strive for on our own. It's a gift from God. Our responsibility is to get in a position to receive.

So, what does this mean for us today? Reflection: How might your life change if you genuinely understood and believed that your heart, the essence of who you are, has been renewed?

Listen, when God promises a new heart, He is referring to a total transformation of your inner self! Just think about it: your very essence, who you truly are, being renewed by the Creator of the universe. Glory to God!

1. Total Transformation: God is in the business of complete renewal. He doesn't just want to tweak your behavior; He wants to change your heart. Praise God!

2. Inside-Out Change: This change happens from the inside out. It's not about trying harder; it's about surrendering to God's transforming power.

3. A New Capacity to Love: When God replaces our stony hearts with hearts of flesh, we become more capable of love, forgiveness, and Christlikeness.

Applying the Promise

How can we position ourselves to receive this new heart and spirit? Here are some practical steps:

1. Acknowledge the Need: Recognize areas where your heart feels hard or unresponsive.

2. Invite God In: Ask God to do the work of transformation in you.

3. Practice Openness: Cultivate a willingness to be changed, even in uncomfortable ways.

4. Engage with God's Word: Regularly read and meditate on Scripture to align your heart with God's.

5. Community: Surround yourself with others who are also seeking heart transformation.

A New You

Remember, friends, no heart is too hard for God to soften. No life is too broken for Him to make new. As we lean into His promise of transformation, let's pray for the courage to let Him do His work in us.

Reflection:

1. In which aspects of your life do you need to embrace the new heart that God has given you?

2. How might your relationships change if you had a soft, responsive heart toward God and others?

3. What's one step you can take today to open yourself up to God's transforming work in your life?

As we continue our journey through this book, keep this promise of a new heart at the forefront of your mind. It's the foundation for us to embrace the practical steps and strategies we'll explore. With God's help, true, lasting change is not just possible—it's promised.

In our next chapter, we will explore the topic of 'metamorphosis' and examine how the transformation of a butterfly closely parallels that of a believer.

CHAPTER 8

METAMORPHOSIS: THE PARALLEL BETWEEN A CATERPILLAR, A BUTTERFLY AND BELIEVERS - PT. 1

One of the most striking examples of transformation in nature is the metamorphosis of a caterpillar into a butterfly. At first glance, the caterpillar seems ordinary—crawling slowly, focused on survival, and entirely unaware of the incredible potential it holds. In many ways, this parallels a new Christian's walk with God: the early stage is filled with promise, yet it also demands a willingness to change and grow beyond what's familiar.

Awareness of Potential

The caterpillar's initial life is all about consuming nourishment and preparing for the journey ahead. Though its world might be limited to nearby leaves and branches, within it lies the blueprint for so much more. Similarly, as believers, we start our spiritual journey with a sense that we are meant for greater things.

The apostle Peter wrote of this divine potential when he reminded early Christians that they were "a chosen people, a royal priesthood, a holy nation" (1 Peter 2:9). This identity points us to a higher calling that requires spiritual growth beyond our present understanding.

The Slow Crawl of Faith

Just as the caterpillar inches along, sometimes at a painstakingly slow pace, our early days in faith often feel like small steps. We might wonder if we'll ever break free from old patterns or misconceptions. Yet, the slowness has purpose. It allows us to become grounded in foundational truths, such as the importance of prayer, Scripture study, and gathering with fellow believers. The Bible encourages this kind of slow, steady progression: "Precept upon precept; line upon line" (Isaiah 28:10). Each spiritual step builds on the last, preparing us for deeper transformation.

Preparing for Change

A caterpillar will eventually stop devouring leaves and, instead, position itself to enter the chrysalis. Though still in the initial stage, it begins to sense that a change must occur—a letting go of its previous existence. Likewise, in the early stages of our Christian journey, God often invites us to surrender what holds us back: old habits, fear, pride, or doubt. When we say yes to this invitation, we're taking the first steps toward genuine transformation. Romans 12:2 reminds us not to conform to the patterns of this world, "but be transformed by the renewing of your mind." This renewal process starts the moment we decide to follow Christ, setting the stage for a deeper metamorphosis.

Spiritual Parallel: A Willing Heart

True transformation requires more than curiosity; it needs a cooperative heart. A caterpillar doesn't resist what comes next—it naturally moves into a state of change. So, too, must the believer. Jesus said, "Abide in me, and I in you" (John 15:4). This abiding posture is like a caterpillar pausing to spin a chrysalis, preparing for an unimaginable future. In the same way, we're called to remain open to God's work in us, trusting that there is far more He intends to do in and through our lives than we can see at the moment.

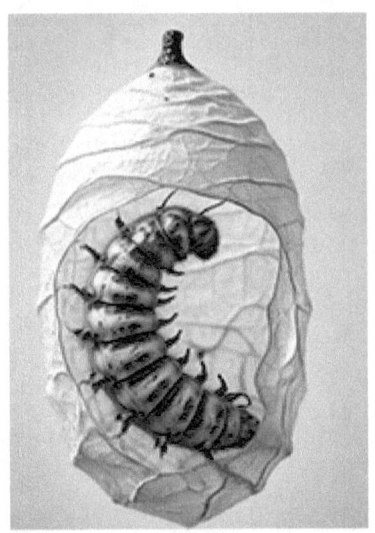

"Free-Will,"

Did you notice in (John 15:4), the verse quoted earlier, that Jesus asks us to *abide*—to remain—in Him? Why does He make this request? It's because we have free will. We can choose to stay with Jesus or walk away from Him. A caterpillar, on-the-other-hand, has no free will; it follows its natural instincts, building a chrysalis and staying within it until its transformation is complete.

For many of us, the challenge arises during the transformational work God is doing in our lives—a process that is rarely comfortable. When faced with discomfort or difficulty, we often exercise our free will and abandon the process before it's complete. As a result, the work remains unfinished and must begin again if or when we return to Him for the completion of the transformational work.

In Part 2 of *Metamorphosis: The Parallel Between a Caterpillar, a Butterfly, and Believers,* we'll complete this powerful analogy. But first, in the next chapter, we'll delve deeper into the incredible gift of free will and how understanding the power of choice can unlock your God-given potential. Together, we'll explore how every decision becomes an opportunity to align with God's purpose and embrace the abundant life He has planned for you.

Let's step into "The Power of Choice."

CHAPTER 9

THE POWER OF CHOICE

Have you ever faced a moment where the weight of a decision felt overwhelming—where you knew your choice could shape your life forever? These are the crossroads that define us, asking questions that stir our hearts: *Do I pursue my own desires, or do I follow what I know is right? Do I stay in the comfort of the familiar, even if it feels far from God, or do I step into the unknown, trusting His plan?*

God, in His infinite love and wisdom, has entrusted us with the incredible gift of free will. This divine gift isn't just a reflection of His love; it's an invitation to walk alongside Him, partnering in His purpose for our lives. Yet, this freedom comes with a sacred responsibility—to choose wisely, to align our decisions with His will, and to trust His ways above our own.

In every moment, you hold the power to decide. Will you follow the path of faith, even when it feels uncertain, trusting that God's way leads to life? The choice is yours. What will you choose?

The Power of Choice

What comes to mind when you think about the power of choice? Is it the freedom to shape your life, or do you envision the weight of responsibility that accompanies each decision? In its simplest form, choice is the ability to decide between options. But in the Christian context, the power of choice takes on a far deeper meaning. It is an invitation to partner with God in shaping our destiny and fulfilling His purpose for our lives.

Choice: The Gift and Responsibility

Choice is one of the greatest gifts God has given humanity. It reflects His image within us, granting us the freedom to align our will with His.

Deuteronomy 30:19 emphasizes this profound truth:

"This day I call the heavens and the earth as witnesses against you that I have set before you life and death, blessings and curses. Now choose life, so that you and your children may live."

This verse reveals that our choices have significant consequences—not just for ourselves, but also for those we influence. Choosing life, in this sense, means choosing God, His ways, and the abundant life He offers through Christ.

Aspects of the Power of Choice

"Every choice you make is a step toward who you are becoming. Choose wisely, guided by love and faith, knowing that when you align with God's ways, you choose a life of peace and purpose." (D.L.S.)

Let's explore the power of choice through its various dimensions. At its core, choice is a reflection of the freedom God has given us. He does not coerce us but lovingly invites us to follow Him.

This freedom allows us to choose salvation, as Joshua declared in Joshua 24:15: "Choose for yourselves this day whom you will serve... But as for me and my household, we will serve the Lord." Choosing God sets us on a path of spiritual transformation anchored in His grace and purpose.

Shaping Our Legacy

Every decision we make contributes to the legacy we leave behind. Whether it's choosing to live with integrity, love unconditionally, or stand firm in faith, our choices ripple outward, influencing our families, communities, and future generations.

As Ruth's decision to follow Naomi led to her becoming part of Christ's lineage, so too can our choices have far-reaching effects.

Daily Dependence on God

While we have the freedom to choose, we are not left to navigate life alone. God promises to guide us when we seek His wisdom. Proverbs 3:5-6 reminds us: "Trust in the Lord with all your heart and lean not on your own understanding; in all your ways submit to him, and he will make your paths straight." Our choices become clearer and more aligned with His will when we lean on Him in prayer and reflection.

Navigating Challenges

The power of choice doesn't mean decisions are always easy. Life often presents us with difficult crossroads where fear, doubt, or external pressures cloud our judgment. Yet even in these moments, we have the choice to trust God's promises, allowing His peace to guide us. Colossians 3:15 encourages us: "Let the peace of Christ rule in your hearts."

Eternal Significance

Ultimately, the power of choice carries eternal weight. Each decision draws us closer to or further from God. Choosing to follow Christ, to obey His Word, and to live a life of faith brings not only abundant life here but also the promise of eternity with Him.

The Role of the Holy Spirit in Our Choices

The power to choose rightly is not based on our strength alone. The Holy Spirit works within us, empowering us to make decisions that honor God. Philippians 2:13 assures us: "For it is God who works in you to will and to act in order to fulfill his good purpose." Through prayer, Scripture, and the Spirit's prompting, we can make choices that reflect His glory and align with His purpose.

Choice: The Pathway to Transformation

Moses captured this truth when he addressed Israel, saying, "I have set before you life and death, blessings and curses. Now choose life, so that you and your children may live" (Deuteronomy 30:19, NIV).

Moses was telling the people of Israel, "God has set before you a path to life and blessings, or you can choose the path of curses and death." Choosing life means more than just existing—it's about thriving in the fullness of God's promises. It's trusting His wisdom over our own, even when the way forward feels uncertain. It's letting go of temporary comfort to embrace eternal purpose.

Moses spoke to the people of Israel with a clear and profound declaration: "God has set before you a path to life and blessings, or you can choose the path of curses and death." This pivotal moment in Deuteronomy

30:19 challenges them—and us—to consider the weight of our choices and the consequences they carry.

Choosing life means far more than mere existence. It's about stepping into the abundance of God's promises and aligning ourselves with His divine purpose. It's choosing to thrive spiritually, emotionally, and relationally by walking in obedience to His Word. Choosing life is an act of trust, a declaration that God's wisdom is greater than our own, even when the path ahead seems unclear or difficult.

This choice often requires courage. It means letting go of the fleeting comforts of this world to embrace the eternal purposes of God. It's about surrendering our fears, doubts, and self-reliance to the One who knows the end from the beginning. As Jesus said in John 10:10, "I have come that they may have life, and have it to the full." Choosing life is stepping into that fullness—a life rich with meaning, joy, and peace that comes from walking in harmony with God's will.

Moses' words come with a solemn warning: the alternative to choosing life is a path marked by disobedience, separation from God, and the pursuit of fleeting gains that ultimately lead to emptiness, curses, and death.

Yet God's desire is not for us to perish but to thrive under His loving care. Therefore, He graciously sets the choice before us and urges us to choose life.

What Does Choosing Life Look Like?

Choosing life begins with a decision to live according to God's commands. In Deuteronomy 30:16, Moses explains, "For I command you today to love the Lord your God, to walk in obedience to him, and to keep his commands, decrees, and laws; then you will live and increase, and the Lord your God will bless you in the land you are entering to possess." Obedience unlocks the blessings and life God has promised.

Trusting God's Plan

Choosing life means trusting God's plan, even when it defies logic or requires waiting. It's about believing that His ways are higher than ours and that His timing is perfect.

Proverbs 3:5-6 encourages us, "Trust in the Lord with all your heart and lean not on your own understanding; in all your ways submit to him, and he will make your paths straight."

Living with Purpose

Choosing life is embracing the purpose God has uniquely designed for each of us. It's about using our gifts, time, and energy to glorify Him and bless others.

This choice not only transforms our own lives but also impacts generations to come.

Surrendering Temporary Comfort

The path of life often requires letting go of what feels safe or familiar to step into the unknown with God. Like Abraham leaving his homeland, choosing life sometimes means sacrificing to pursue God's greater purpose.

This surrender is not a loss but a trade—temporary comfort for eternal significance.

The Invitation to Choose Life

Moses' words echo through the centuries, offering us the same invitation today: "Now choose life, so that you and your children may live" (Deuteronomy 30:19, NIV). The choice is ours to make. Will we follow the path that leads to life and blessings, trusting God's wisdom and walking in His promises? Or will we settle for a life of compromise, chasing fleeting comforts that ultimately lead to death?

The path of life is one of joy, purpose, and eternal hope. It's a choice that requires faith, surrender, and obedience, but the rewards are beyond measure. God stands ready to walk with us every step of the way. Let us boldly choose life and step into the fullness of all that He has prepared for us.

What about you? What "life" choices is God calling you to make today? Are there areas where you've settled for less than His best? Have you chosen fear over faith or comfort over growth? His call is clear: Choose life. Step into His plans, embrace His transformation, and boldly walk into the future He has prepared for you. This is the best decision you can make.

Decision Making: The Power of Choice and Commitment

Here's the thing about decisions: they require commitment. Let's examine the origin of the word "decision." The word "decision" originates from the Latin term "decisio," which means "a cutting off" or "a settling." This, in turn, comes from the Latin verb "decidere," formed from two parts:

De- means "off" or "away from."
Caedere meaning "to cut."

Together, "decidere" conveys the idea of cutting away alternatives to arrive at a choice or conclusion. This etymology emphasizes the decisive action of eliminating other possibilities to focus on a single path, aligning with the concept of making a clear and committed choice.

A decision goes beyond casual selection; it is a conscious act of will. It involves choosing a path and shutting out others, fully dedicating your energy and focus to the journey that lies ahead.

Think of a man proposing to the woman he loves. In that moment, he's choosing her above all others, declaring his intention to build a life together. When she says yes, she makes her own commitment, letting go of other possibilities to embrace a shared future. True transformation demands the same intentionality and resolve.

But how often do we allow indecision to hold us back? How many dreams and opportunities have slipped through our fingers because we hesitated to make a choice? Indecision is a silent thief, whispering doubts, feeding fears, and convincing us to delay until the "perfect" moment.

Overcoming Indecision

In the next chapter, we'll explore deeper into the dangers of indecision. You'll learn how it creeps into our lives unnoticed, how it affects every area of our being, and—most importantly—how to overcome it. Through practical steps and biblical principles, you'll discover how to break free from the paralysis of indecision and step boldly into God's plan for your life.

The time to act is now. Turn the page and learn how to overcome "indecision," a silent thief...

CHAPTER 10

INDECISION: THE SILENT THIEF OF DREAMS AND OPPORTUNITIES

THE PERILS OF INDECISION

Indecision isn't just about taking a moment to think—it's a quiet force that can slow you down and steal opportunities. Whether it's deciding how to spend your day or making a big decision like starting a new career or relationship, staying stuck can lead to missed chances, added stress, and even feeling distant from God. When we hesitate too long, we risk delaying the plans He has for us.

As believers, we're called to walk boldly in faith, trusting God's direction for our lives. Yet, the fear of making the wrong choice or the uncertainty of what lies ahead often traps us in a cycle of overthinking. **We may even start doubting our ability to hear God's voice clearly.** This hesitation can prevent us from stepping into the plans God has prepared for us.

In this chapter, we will uncover the reasons behind indecision, explore how it affects your life, and learn how aligning your choices with God's wisdom can bring clarity, confidence, and purpose.

We will also discuss practical steps you can take right now to replace hesitation with determination. It's time to break free and move forward in faith!

Understanding Indecision

Indecision is the inability—or sometimes the unwillingness—to make a definitive choice. It's often marked by hesitation, doubt, or an overwhelming fear of choosing incorrectly. This state of uncertainty creates internal conflict, leaving a person unable to commit to a course of action or take decisive steps forward.

The root causes of indecision can vary widely. It may stem from a fear of failure, where the possibility of a wrong choice feels paralyzing. It could be fueled by over-analyzing options, endlessly weighing pros and cons to the point of exhaustion. A lack of self-confidence might leave someone doubting their ability to make the right decision, while a desire to avoid potential consequences can lead to avoidance altogether.

Indecision is more than hesitation—it's a mental and emotional state that stalls progress, causes missed opportunities, and hinders personal growth, relationships, and goals. It isn't just the lack of a decision, but often a deliberate or unconscious choice to avoid making one.

The Cost of Indecision

Indecision may appear harmless at first—a pause to consider your options. But over time, its toll becomes undeniable. Missed opportunities, weakened relationships, and stalled spiritual growth are just the beginning. Some have even lost their health, finances, or families because they hesitated when decisive action was needed.

One striking example of indecision's cost comes from the downfall of Blockbuster, a name once synonymous with movie nights and family traditions.

Blockbuster's Fatal Flaw

In the waning days of Blockbuster's dominance, a meeting took place in their corporate office. The entertainment industry was changing rapidly, with streaming services like Netflix on the rise. Sarah, a visionary executive, urged the company to invest in a streaming platform.

"We need to adapt," she insisted. "This is the future."

But the CEO hesitated. Blockbuster's legacy was built on the in-store experience—the thrill of browsing aisles and the nostalgia of physical movie rentals. Could they risk everything on a model that felt impersonal and uncertain?

While Blockbuster wavered, competitors surged ahead. By the time they launched their own streaming service, the damage was done. The empire crumbled under debt and shifting consumer habits. Stores closed, shelves gathered dust, and what was once a household name became a cautionary tale.

Reflecting on the company's demise, the CEO admitted that his indecision had cost Blockbuster its future. The reluctance to adapt and take bold risks allowed competitors to flourish while they fell behind. The lesson was clear: recognizing the need for change isn't enough—acting with courage and urgency is essential to avoid becoming paralyzed by fear and uncertainty.

Indecision: The Silent Thief of Dreams and Opportunities

The story of Blockbuster's rise and fall isn't just a cautionary tale for businesses—it's a powerful reminder of how indecision can rob us of opportunities in every area of life. Whether in relationships, careers, or faith, the inability to act at crucial moments can have lasting consequences. Let's explore how indecision—hesitating to take action—affects these vital areas.

How Indecision Harms Relationships, Business, and Faith

Indecision is often subtle, creeping into our lives and silently eroding what matters most. It may feel like harmless hesitation, but over time, it can damage relationships, derail careers, and stall spiritual growth.

Relationships: The Deterioration of Connection

Indecision can be just as harmful in relationships as it is in business. When couples avoid tough conversations, fail to address conflicts, or neglect to discuss their different goals, they often drift apart. This situation is similar to what Blockbuster faced in the early 2000s. While the video rental industry was changing, companies like Netflix embraced new trends and adapted. Blockbuster, however, clung to the familiar and hesitated to change, leading to its downfall.

In a relationship, one partner might be ready for change and growth, while the other feels comfortable staying the same. This difference can create tension as their goals and visions for the future move further apart. Without honest communication and a willingness to address these issues, the relationship can suffer from unresolved problems.

Indecision often shows itself in different ways. It might mean avoiding serious discussions about important topics like marriage, children, or career plans. It could also mean ignoring conflicts instead of working through them in a healthy way. Sometimes, indecision comes from a fear of change or a lack of understanding about personal needs and desires.

When these issues remain unresolved, they can harm the relationship. Resentment can grow, trust and intimacy can fade, and couples might begin to drift apart emotionally, even while living together. Over time, these unaddressed problems can lead to the end of the relationship.

To avoid this, couples must focus on honest and open communication. This means having the courage to talk about difficult topics, listening to each other's perspectives, and working together to find solutions. When both partners commit to mutual respect and personal growth, they can build a stronger and healthier relationship.

Taking Decisive Actions in a Relationship

Decisive action in a relationship demands awareness, flexibility, and adaptability. Just as businesses must pivot in response to changing market conditions, couples must be open to adjusting their course as their circumstances and priorities evolve. This may involve compromising, finding creative solutions, or even redefining the terms of the relationship.

Ultimately, the key to maintaining a solid, healthy relationship in the face of indecision is a shared commitment to growth and a willingness to prioritize the partnership above individual preferences. By approaching challenges as a team, communicating openly and honestly, and being decisive in the face of difficult choices, couples can navigate the ups and downs of life together, emerging stronger and more united on the other side.

Business: Missed Opportunities

The challenges and opportunities in the world of small businesses are clear. In a rapidly evolving economy, entrepreneurs face a crossroads where adaptability and agility are essential. They must be courageous enough to change direction, welcome new technologies, and embrace changing consumer preferences.

Consider a neighborhood bookstore that hesitates to create an online presence or a local eatery that resists offering delivery services. These small businesses resemble Blockbuster in their industries—sticking to outdated models and ignoring the need for change.

However, within these moments lie important lessons and new opportunities. The bookstore that wants to connect with readers online and the restaurant looking to deliver their food are on the brink of transformation. They have the potential for growth and resilience in a changing landscape.

Decisive Actions in Business

Small businesses must be ready to adapt and innovate if they want to have or maintain a successful business. In today's dynamic market, the ability to pivot and embrace change is not just a survival tactic—it's a growth strategy. The rapid pace of technological advancements, shifting consumer preferences, and emerging competitors means that standing still is no longer an option. Businesses that thrive are those that remain proactive, identifying opportunities before they become necessities.

Innovation doesn't always require massive changes; even small adjustments can yield significant results. For instance, enhancing customer engagement through personalized experiences or exploring new delivery methods can set a business apart from its competition. Similarly, adapting to trends like sustainability or leveraging digital tools can help businesses remain relevant and appealing to their target audience.

Adaptation also means being willing to let go of strategies that no longer serve the business. This may involve retiring outdated products, revising marketing tactics, or streamlining operations. By maintaining a mindset of continuous improvement, businesses can not only weather disruptions but also uncover new avenues for growth and profitability.

The willingness to adapt and innovate is the hallmark of a resilient business. It's about anticipating changes, embracing challenges, and transforming them into opportunities for success.

Faith: The Struggle with Belief

Indecision can also affect one's spiritual journey. Decisive action is not just important—it's essential—for spiritual growth. Many of us feel a call to deepen our commitment, develop a closer relationship with God, or live out our values more fully in the world. Yet, this journey often requires us to step outside our comfort zones, confront our doubts and fears, and take bold steps in new directions.

Decisive Actions in Faith

Being decisive in our spiritual pursuits means making intentional choices to grow in faith. It's like planting and nurturing a seed with care, knowing that it will eventually blossom into something beautiful and strong. This requires a commitment to prioritize actions that deepen our connection with God and align our lives with His purpose.

This could mean dedicating time each day to prayer or meditation, where we intentionally quiet our minds and open our hearts to God's guidance. It might involve joining a Bible study or fellowship group to learn, share, and grow alongside others who are on similar journeys. Being decisive in our faith also calls us to reflect on how we live out our values, choosing kindness, integrity, and love in our daily interactions.

Every choice we make, whether small or significant, contributes to our spiritual growth. Like a gardener tending a plant, we must consistently water our faith with acts of devotion, prune away distractions, and let the light of God's Word shine on us. In doing so, we allow our spiritual lives to flourish, becoming rooted in strength and producing fruit that blesses both ourselves and those around us.

The Universal Cost of Indecision

The danger of indecision is universal: it delays progress, breeds anxiety, erodes trust, and ultimately leads to stagnation. Like Blockbuster, we may find ourselves paralyzed by fear, clinging to what feels safe, only to discover that the cost of inaction far outweighs the risks of change. The world doesn't wait, and neither does God's purpose for our lives.

Three Main Causes of Indecision

1. **Fear of Failure:** Fear of making a wrong choice can be paralyzing. But remember, 2 Timothy 1:7 says, "For God has not given us a spirit of fear, but of power and of love and of a sound mind." Trusting in God's strength can help us move past our fears.

2. **Lack of Clarity:** Not knowing or understanding what you should do can make it hard to decide. Proverbs 3:5-6 advises us to "Trust in the Lord with all your heart, and lean not on your own understanding; in all your ways acknowledge Him, and He shall direct your paths." Through prayer, the leading of the Holy Spirit, and wisdom from trusted spiritual leaders, you can receive wise counsel to guide you in your decisions.

3. **Fear of Judgment:** A big reason we can't make decisions is the fear of being judged. We worry about how others will see our choices and whether they will approve or criticize us. This fear can make us hesitate and stop us from making firm decisions.

Confronting Indecision

As previously stated, indecision is a thief that quietly steals our dreams and robs us of countless opportunities. It can keep us stuck in a state of stagnation, preventing us from reaching our full potential. Like a robber, indecision creeps into our lives, slowly eroding our confidence and hindering our ability to take decisive action.

When confronting indecision, it's vital to remember that God equips us with everything we need to make wise and confident choices. Fear of failure, lack of clarity, and fear of judgment may feel overwhelming, but they don't have to dominate your decision-making process. God's Word provides a roadmap, reminding us to rely on His strength, seek His guidance, and trust His direction.

When fear arises, let 2 Timothy 1:7 remind you of the spirit of power, love, and soundness of mind that God has already placed within you. When clarity feels elusive, lean into Proverbs 3:5-6, trusting in the Lord to illuminate your path. And when fear of judgment clouds your confidence, remember that your worth and identity are found in Christ, not in the opinions of others.

Overcoming Indecision

To overcome indecision, we first need to identify its root causes. Indecision doesn't occur randomly; it arises from deeper fears, doubts, and beliefs that hold us back. It's essential to confront these feelings by asking yourself three key questions and answering them truthfully.

1. **"Why am I indecisive?"**

   ○ This is a question of self-awareness. What lies beneath your hesitation? Are you afraid of making the wrong choice? Do you fear failure or judgment? Sometimes, indecision is rooted in perfectionism—the belief that every decision must be flaw-less—or in past experiences where choices led to unfavorable outcomes. Be honest with yourself and explore what's truly holding you back.

2. **"What am I afraid of?"**

   ○ Fear is often the root of indecision—whether it's fear of failure, fear of the unknown, or even fear of success. This fear can keep you stuck, unable to move forward. Take a moment to reflect: *What am I avoiding by staying in this place of limbo?* Is it the possibility of making a mistake? The discomfort that comes with change?

   ○ Identifying your fears is the first step to overcoming them. Once you recognize what's holding you back, you can confront those fears and surrender them to God. Remember the truth of 2 Timothy 1:7:
   "For God has not given us a spirit of fear, but of power and of love and of a sound mind."

   ○ God's Spirit within you gives you the strength to move forward with courage, love, and clear thinking. Trust Him to help you face your fears and take the next step toward the life He's calling you to. Fear is often the root of indecision—whether it's fear of failure, fear of the unknown, or even fear of success. This fear can keep you stuck, unable to move forward. Take a moment to reflect: *What am I avoiding by staying in this place of limbo?* Is it the possibility of making a mistake? The discomfort that comes with change?

- Identifying your fears is the first step to overcoming them. Once you recognize what's holding you back, you can confront those fears and surrender them to God. Remember the truth of 2 Timothy 1:7:
  "For God has not given us a spirit of fear, but of power and of love and of a sound mind."

- God's Spirit within you gives you the strength to move forward with courage, love, and clear thinking. Trust Him to help you face your fears and take the next step toward the life He's calling you to.

3. "What do I truly want?"

- Indecision often arises from conflicting desires. Take the time to clarify your goals and priorities. What outcome are you hoping for? What matters most to you in this situation? By aligning your desires with your values and God's will for your life, you can gain the clarity needed to make confident decisions.

The Path Forward

Overcoming indecision begins with a single step—no matter how small. Once you've identified the root causes, it's time to take intentional action. Start by committing your plans to God through prayer, seeking His guidance and direction.

The Bible assures us in James 1:5:

"If any of you lacks wisdom, you should ask God, who gives generously to all without finding fault, and it will be given to you."

God's wisdom is always available, and He delights in leading those who seek Him. Trust Him to guide your steps as you move forward in faith. Each act of obedience, no matter how small, brings you closer to His purpose for your life. Let go of fear, embrace His promises, and take that first step today.

In an upcoming chapter, we'll explore the topic of how to be decisive. However, before that, I'd like to share a few stories about individuals who conquered their indecision and found success.

Prepare to bolster your faith as you explore the "Success Stories of Contemporary Christian Individuals."

CHAPTER 11

SUCCESS STORIES OF MODERN-DAY CHRISTIANS WHO OVERCAME INDECISION

Here are stories from contemporary Christian individuals whose struggles with making decisions significantly affected their lives and businesses. Their honest accounts reveal how indecision delayed their success and how faith guided them back to clarity and purpose.

Dave Ramsey's Story: From Collapse to Clarity

Dave Ramsey, now a household name in Christian financial advising, wasn't always a success story. In fact, he began his career as a promising real estate investor, but his inability to make firm financial decisions brought him to the brink of ruin. Ramsey describes this season in his life in his book, The Total Money Makeover: "I was having some success in real estate, but in an effort to keep leveraging and growing, I took on too much debt. Foreclosure, lawsuits, and potential bankruptcy loomed over my head."

Ramsey found himself at a painful crossroads. Torn between continuing risky financial strategies for growth and adopting a conservative approach to money management, his indecision paralyzed him. The pressure mounted as his financial troubles spiraled. "I was scared to death," he recalls. "I felt the weight of responsibility bearing down on me, and I knew things were spiraling out of control." Ramsey's rock-bottom moment forced him to confront the choices that had brought him to this crisis.

Desperate for direction, Ramsey turned to Scripture and found clarity in Proverbs 22:7: "The rich rule over the poor, and the borrower is slave to the lender." This truth transformed his perspective. By committing to biblical financial principles and abandoning his double-mindedness, he made a decisive shift to conservative money management. The outcome? Ramsey rebuilt his financial life and founded Financial Peace University, which has since empowered millions with practical, biblical financial wisdom. His story reminds us that clarity and faith lead to freedom and purpose.

Reflection Questions:

How can you apply Ramsey's lessons to your financial decisions? In what areas of your life do you struggle with double-mindedness? What biblical principles can guide you toward making more decisive choices?

Kari Jobe's Story: From Hesitation to Calling

Kari Jobe, now a Grammy-nominated Christian artist, began her journey torn between two paths. Early in her career, she wavered between the safety of counseling—a predictable and stable career—and her passion for music ministry. "I was hesitant to fully commit to music, seeing counseling as the 'safe' choice," she shared in an interview with Relevant Magazine. But this hesitation came at a cost, leaving her talents underdeveloped and her true calling unfulfilled.

During this season of indecision, Kari turned to her father, a pastor, for wisdom. He posed a powerful question inspired by the story of Elijah:

"How long will you waver between two opinions?" (1 Kings 18:21). This deeply resonated with Kari, and she realized her indecision was keeping her from fully stepping into God's plan for her life. She wrestled with fear—fear of failure, of rejection, and of the unknown.

With her father's guidance and God's conviction, Kari made the bold decision to dedicate herself fully to music ministry. This commitment freed her from the chains of hesitation and allowed her to pursue her calling wholeheartedly. Since then, Kari's albums and songs have inspired millions, bearing fruit that only came from her willingness to trust God and embrace her purpose. Her story shows the power of decisiveness in unlocking the blessings of God.

Reflection Questions:

What are the "two opinions" you find yourself wavering between in your life? How can seeking wisdom from trusted mentors help you overcome indecision? What fears hold you back from fully embracing your calling?

William McDowell's Story:

From Fear to Faith, William McDowell, a celebrated gospel artist, faced his own battle with indecision. As a worship leader at his church, McDowell felt a dual calling—to continue serving in his secure role or to take the leap of faith into a full-time music career. For a long time, he was stuck. "I felt a deep calling to spread the gospel through music," he shared, "but I was afraid of leaving the security of my church position."

McDowell's fears held him captive. What if he failed? What if he misheard God's call? The weight of these questions left him paralyzed. It wasn't until a time of prayer, encouraged by his pastor, that McDowell found clarity. He described the turning point: "I realized that my fear was holding me back from what God had planned for me. I needed to trust Him fully." That revelation brought him face-to-face with the truth: faith requires action, even when the outcome is uncertain.

Once McDowell embraced this clarity, he pursued his music career wholeheartedly. The decision unlocked a wave of blessings—he released multiple successful albums that have ministered to believers worldwide. His story shows the power of stepping out in faith and trusting God's plan, even when the path feels risky.

Reflection Questions:

What secure roles in your life are you hesitant to leave for a higher calling? How can prayer and spiritual guidance help you overcome fears related to decision-making? What steps can you take today to trust God more fully with your future? The Universal Message: Overcoming Indecision Dave Ramsey, Kari Jobe, and William McDowell each faced critical moments where indecision threatened to derail their purpose. Yet through prayer, biblical guidance, and bold action, they broke free from the grip of hesitation and stepped into their God-given calling.

What about you? Are there areas in your life where indecision has held you back? Have you been stuck between the comfort of what's familiar and the call to something greater? These stories remind us that the path to clarity starts with seeking God, trusting His plan, and taking that first courageous step.

As the apostle James reminds us, "A double-minded man is unstable in all his ways" (James 1:8, KJV). Indecision keeps us stuck, robbing us of the peace, clarity, and purpose God desires for us. But it doesn't have to be this way. When you seek Him, pray for wisdom, and trust His guidance, you'll find the strength to step boldly into the life He has prepared for you.

Key Takeaways:

Seek Divine Guidance: Turn to Scripture and prayer when facing difficult decisions. Trust in God's Plan: Believe that God has a purpose for your life and that He will guide you.

Take Bold Steps: Move forward in faith, even when the outcome is uncertain. Your breakthrough begins with a single, decisive step—a made-up mind that says, "Yes, Lord, I will trust You."

In the upcoming chapter, as promised, we will focus on how to "be decisive." We'll delve into making bold, faith-driven choices and how to walk confidently in alignment with God's plan.

Prepare to break free from the cycle of indecision and embrace ' Decisiveness', Through 'The Power of a Made-Up Mind.' It's time to turn the page on Indecision.

CHAPTER 12

DECISIVENESS: THE POWER OF A MADE-UP MIND

Decisiveness is the ability to make decisions deliberately, with purpose, and effectively, producing confidence in the outcome. It means acting boldly and swiftly, seizing opportunities rather than hesitating in the face of uncertainty.

"The path to success is paved with bold, timely, and decisive actions."

In this chapter, we will explore the power of decisiveness, examine the obstacles that hinder our ability to make firm decisions, and uncover how a resolute, made-up mind can transform our lives.

While the ability to make bold decisions is vital, what's even more crucial is having the unwavering determination to stick with those decisions, no matter the challenges or adversities we encounter.

Unfortunately, many people make decisions that are right or beneficial, only to waver or give up when pressure arises. They allow adversity to erode their resolve, ultimately abandoning the path they set out on.

Having a made-up mind is an essential first step in the decision-making process, but equally important is ensuring that our decisions are wholehearted and fully committed. It is this full-hearted commitment that empowers us to endure challenges, push through resistance, and stay the course until we see the fruits of our resolve.

I want to share a story with you from the Bible about the cost of half-hearted decisions. This story highlights the importance of not only making the right choice but also fully committing to it, regardless of the obstacles that arise along the way. It serves as a powerful reminder that following through with unwavering faith can make all the difference in the outcome of our lives.

The Cost of Half-Hearted Decisions

Decisions are pivotal—they mark the turning points of our lives. But the story doesn't end when the decision is made. The true impact is determined by our follow-through. The Bible offers many examples of people who made bold decisions but faltered along the way. Among them is Peter, whose decision to step out of the boat and walk on water toward Jesus in the midst of a storm offers a profound lesson for all of us.

The Moment of Faith

The scene unfolds in Matthew 14:22-33 (KJV). Jesus had sent the disciples ahead of Him, and as they sailed across the sea, a violent storm arose. In the darkest hours of the night, Jesus came to them, walking on water. The disciples were terrified, mistaking Him for a ghost. But Jesus spoke calming words: *"Be of good cheer; it is I; be not afraid"* (Matthew 14:27).

Peter, bold and impulsive as ever, responded: *"Lord, if it be thou, bid me come unto thee on the water."* Jesus said, *"Come."* With those words, Peter made a decision—a bold decision to leave the safety of the boat and step out into the unknown by faith, trusting Jesus completely.

The Midway Crisis

At first, Peter's faith carried him. He defied natural law, walking on water toward Jesus. But then, something changed. The wind howled louder, the waves grew larger, and Peter's focus shifted.

Instead of fixing his eyes on Jesus, Peter began to fixate on the adversity around him. Fear crept in, his faith wavered, and he began to sink.

Peter's choice to take a leap of faith on a stormy sea was admirable. He acted when the other Elven disciples of Jesus hesitated. If Peter had focused solely on Jesus, the storm, the waves, and the threats wouldn't have affected him. We only stumble when we take our eyes/focus off of Jesus, the Word of God, and our identity as children of God.

Peter cried out, *"Lord, save me!"* And immediately, Jesus stretched out His hand and caught him, asking, *"O thou of little faith, wherefore didst thou doubt?"*

Lessons Learned from Peter's Struggles with Faith

1. **A Bold Decision Alone Is Not Enough:**
   Peter's initial choice was based on faith and bravery. However, a decision made during a moment of spiritual clarity needs to be supported by ongoing trust and perseverance. It's simple to make firm commitments when we are inspired, but the challenges of life will reveal whether we genuinely stand by them.

2. **Adversity Is Inevitable**
   When Peter stepped out of the boat, the storm didn't stop. Often, we assume that obedience will result in instant calm. But faith is not the absence of storms; it is the ability to walk through them

with confidence in God's power.

3. **Focus Determines Outcomes**

The moment Peter took his eyes off Jesus, his faith gave way to fear. This is true in our lives as well. When we focus on our circumstances—the challenges, the critics, the uncertainties—we sink under the weight of doubt. But when our eyes remain fixed on Jesus, we find the strength to move forward.

4. **God's Grace Meets Us in Our Weakness**

Even when Peter faltered, Jesus was there. He didn't let Peter drown. In the same way, God's grace is sufficient for us, even when our faith wavers. He reaches out His hand to lift us up, reminding us that He is the source of our strength.

The Danger of Midway Commitment Changes

How often do we make decisions but fail to follow through? Perhaps we resolve to deepen our prayer life, but distractions pull us away. Or we commit to a new direction in life, but the challenges make us second-guess our choice. Like Peter, we step out with great intentions, but midway through, we falter.

Midway commitment changes are costly. It leaves us vulnerable, exposed to fear, doubt, and defeat. It robs us of the blessings that come from completing the journey. Imagine if Peter had kept walking, reaching Jesus, and standing firm with Him on the water. The testimony of his faith would have been even greater.

Moving Forward in Faith

If you find yourself sinking like Peter, remember these steps to regain your footing:

1. **Refocus on Jesus**

   No matter how far you've strayed, it's never too late to turn your eyes back to Him. Like Peter, cry out, *"Lord, save me!"* He will always respond.

2. **Renew Your Commitment**

   Don't let the storm talk you out of your decision. Revisit why you stepped out in the first place and trust that Jesus is still calling you forward.

3. **Take the Next Step**

   Faith isn't about leaping to the finish line; it's about taking the next step, even when the waves seem insurmountable.

4. **Rely on His Strength:**

   Peter couldn't walk on water in his own strength, and neither can we. Whatever God has called you to, He will equip you to accomplish it.

The Call to Complete the Journey

When God calls you out of the boat, He doesn't expect perfection—He expects perseverance. The storms will come, but His presence will sustain you. Don't let fear or doubt cause you to sink. Keep your eyes on Jesus, and trust Him to carry you through.

Remember: a decision is only as powerful as the faith and action that follow it. Peter's story reminds us that even when we falter, God's hand is ready to catch us. But let it also inspire us to keep moving forward, unwavering in our trust, until we reach the One who called us out in the first place.

James 1:8 tells us, "A double-minded man is unstable in all his ways" (KJV). This instability creates tension not just in one area of life, but across them all. Double-mindedness leads to confusion, hesitation, and missed opportunities. But God does not call us to live in confusion. He calls us to boldness, anchored in His unchanging truth.

The Power of a Made-Up Mind

A made-up mind doesn't mean you'll have all the answers or a clear map of the future. It means you are fully committed to following God's guidance, even when the way forward seems uncertain. Take Joshua as an example. After Moses' death, Joshua was tasked with leading the Israelites into the Promised Land. God's command to him was clear: "Be strong and very courageous... do not turn from [the law] to the right, or, to the left, that you may be successful wherever you go" (Joshua 1:7, NIV).

Joshua's success came from trusting God's plan and moving forward with unwavering faith. He didn't let fear or doubt paralyze him; he chose action over hesitation and faith over fear.

After the Israelites entered the Promised Land and received significant wealth and property through conquest, fulfilling God's promise, many of the tribes turned away from Him and seek after other gods. Need motivated their relationship with God, not love. Once they felt secure and prosperous in the land, they no longer perceived a need for God in their lives.

In contrast, Joshua remained steadfast in his devotion to God, continuously meditating on His word. Joshua boldly challenged those who had forsaken God, declaring: "But if serving the Lord seems undesirable to you, then choose for yourselves this day whom you will serve, whether the gods your ancestors served beyond the Euphrates, or the gods of the Amorites, in whose land you are living. But as for me and my household, we will serve the Lord."

Joshua had 'a made-up mind'. Success, failure, wealth, or poverty wouldn't change his relationship with God. By meditating on God's word, Joshua gained a moral compass that prevented him from going astray.

Imagine how your unwavering commitment to serve God can significantly affect your family. Consider how your example and influence could touch and transform countless lives for eternity.

Overcoming Obstacles to Decision-Making

Decision-making is an essential part of life, yet it is often one of the most challenging tasks we face. Whether it's a major life choice or a seemingly simple daily decision, obstacles like fear, uncertainty, doubt, and external pressures can cloud our judgment and leave us feeling stuck. These hurdles can make the process feel overwhelming, causing us to second-guess ourselves or avoid making decisions altogether.

However, overcoming these obstacles is crucial for personal growth and living a purposeful life. Each decision we make shapes the direction of our journey, influencing not only our lives but also the lives of those around us. The key is to confront the barriers head-on, equipping ourselves with wisdom, faith, and practical tools to navigate the decision-making process with clarity and confidence.

The Process of Overcoming Obstacles to Decision-Making

As we explore overcoming these obstacles, it's important to acknowledge that challenges are a natural part of decision-making. Even the most decisive individuals encounter moments of hesitation or doubt. What sets them apart is their ability to navigate through those moments rather than becoming paralyzed by them. They understand every obstacle presents an opportunity to grow in wisdom and trust in God's plan.

Let's address three of the most common challenges faced in decision-making.

1. **Fear of Failure**

   Fear often asks, "What if I make the wrong choice?" or "What if I fail?" These questions can paralyze you. But even when mistakes are made, God can use them for good. Isaiah 41:10 reminds us, "Do not fear, for I am with you... I will strengthen you and help you; I will uphold you with my righteous right hand" (NIV). Trusting in God allows you to face decisions with courage, knowing He is with you.

2. **Overthinking**

   Over-analyzing can feel like productivity, but it often leads to procrastination. Proverbs 3:5-6 advises, "Trust in the Lord with all your heart and lean not on your own understanding... he will make your paths straight" (NIV). Trust God, even when the details remain unclear.

3. **Fear of Disapproval**

Decisions driven by the desire to please others often lead to frustration. Galatians 1:10 reminds us, "If I were still trying to please people, I would not be a servant of Christ" (NIV). Seek to please God, and you'll find true freedom.

Mastering Confident Decision Making

To confidently make decisions, follow these five steps:

- **Clarify Your Goals and Values**

  Begin by identifying what truly matters to you. What are your ultimate goals, and how do they align with your values and faith? Clear priorities serve as a compass, helping you evaluate options and stay focused on what's most important. Proverbs 16:9 reminds us, "In their hearts, humans plan their course, but the Lord establishes their steps" (NIV). When your goals align with God's purpose, your path becomes clearer.

- **Gather Information and Weigh Your Options**

  A confident decision is an informed decision. Take time to gather relevant facts, consider the pros and cons, and consult trusted sources. Whether it's seeking advice from a mentor, conducting research, or praying for wisdom, preparation equips you to choose wisely. James 1:5 encourages us, "If any of you lacks wisdom, you should ask God, who gives generously to all without finding fault, and it will be given to you" (NIV).

- **Seek God's Guidance Through Prayer:**

  Prayer is a powerful tool for decision-making. Invite God into the process and ask for clarity, peace, and confirmation. Spend time in quiet reflection, listening for the Holy Spirit's guidance. Philippians 4:6-7 assures us that when we present our requests to God with thanksgiving, His peace will guard our hearts and minds.

- **Take a Step of Faith**

  Once you've clarified your goals, gathered information, and sought God's guidance, it's time to act. Fear and uncertainty may linger, but faith requires moving forward despite them. Trust that God will honor your effort and guide your steps. As Proverbs 3:5-6 advises, "Trust in the Lord with all your heart and lean not on your own understanding; in all your ways submit to him, and he will make your paths straight" (NIV).

- **Reflect and Adjust as Needed**

  Decision-making doesn't end once you've made a choice. Take time to reflect on the outcomes and assess whether they align with your goals and God's purpose. Be willing to make adjustments if necessary. Mistakes are not failures; they are opportunities for growth and refinement. Romans 8:28 reminds us that "in all things God works for the good of those who love him, who have been called according to his purpose" (NIV).

By following these steps, you can approach decisions with confidence and peace, knowing that you are seeking God's will and making choices that align with His purpose for your life.

The Advantages of Being Decisive

A decisive life is a focused life. The apostle Paul illustrated this when he said, "Forgetting what is behind and straining toward what is ahead, I press on toward the goal to win the prize for which God has called me heavenward in Christ Jesus" (Philippians 3:13-14, NIV). Like Paul, you can move forward with boldness, focused on the prize God has set before you.

Decisions are the building blocks of transformation. But true change begins within—at the level of your thoughts and beliefs.

As we move into the next chapter, *The Renewing of the Mind*, we'll explore how aligning your mindset with God's truth not only empowers your decisions, but also transforms your life from the inside out.

CHAPTER 13

RENEWING THE MIND: THE FOUNDATION OF TRANSFORMATION

The concept of renewing the mind is one of the most powerful principles for personal and spiritual transformation. The apostle Paul, in his letter to the Romans, writes, *"Do not conform to the pattern of this world, but be transformed by the renewing of your mind"* (Romans 12:2, NIV). These words remind us that true change doesn't come from simply altering our outward behavior; it begins within, through the reshaping of how we think and perceive the world.

Understanding the Mind's Role in Transformation

The mind serves as a remarkable processing center, constantly interpreting our experiences, shaping our beliefs, and influencing how we respond to life's challenges. What we dwell on in our thoughts impacts our emotions, choices, and, ultimately, the direction of our lives. This is why the renewal of our mind is not just helpful, but essential for lasting transformation.

Imagine your mind as a computer. Like a computer processes information based on its programming, our minds operate according to the "programming" we've accumulated over time—through experiences, cultural influences, and even personal habits. But what happens when a computer's software becomes outdated or corrupted? It slows down, malfunctions, or even crashes. In the same way, old and unhealthy thought patterns can hinder our ability to live in alignment with God's will and purpose for our lives.

Three Steps to Renewing Your Thought Patterns

1. Recognize Unhealthy Thought Patterns

The first step in renewing your mind is recognizing the thought patterns you currently follow. This requires honest self-reflection and a willingness to confront beliefs that don't align with God's truth. Think of it like a gardener tending to a garden: before removing weeds, the gardener must first identify them. In the same way, you must acknowledge unhealthy thoughts before you can replace them. Ask yourself, "Do my thoughts reflect faith, hope, and love, or do they lean toward fear, doubt, and negativity?"

2. Replace False Beliefs with Truth

Once you've identified unhealthy thoughts, the next step is to replace them with truth. This process happens through regular engagement with God's Word. Scripture acts as a compass, guiding us toward truth and helping us discern what is real from what is false. When you encounter a thought that goes against biblical truth—such as feelings of unworthiness or fear—reject it and replace it with God's perspective. For example, if you're tempted to think, *"I can't do this,"* counter it with the truth found in Philippians 4:13: *"I can do all this through Him who gives me strength"* (NIV).

3. Practice New Thought Patterns

Finally, renewing your mind requires consistent practice. Just as repeated actions build muscle memory, repeated thoughts strengthen neural pathways in the brain. By continually choosing to think in alignment with

God's truth, you create new mental habits that reflect His perspective. This is not an instant transformation, but a gradual process. Each time you choose truth over lies, you reinforce patterns of thinking that honor God and bring peace to your heart.

Take these steps one day at a time, trusting that God is with you on the journey. Remember, transformation is not just about changing what you think—it's about aligning your mind with the truth of God's Word, allowing Him to renew and reshape your life from the inside out.

Practical Steps for Mind Renewal

To implement this process effectively, consider these practical steps:

1. Daily Scripture Meditation: Set aside a specific time each day to read and reflect on God's Word. Rather than rushing through passages, choose a small portion and think deeply about its implications for your life.

2. Thought Monitoring: Throughout the day, practice catching and examining your thoughts. Ask yourself: "Is this thought true according to God's Word? Is it helpful? Is it necessary?"

3. Truth Declaration: When you identify negative or false thoughts, immediately counter them with relevant Scripture. Speaking truth aloud can be particularly effective in this process.

4. Environmental Management: Carefully choose what you allow to influence your thinking. This includes being selective about media consumption, relationships, and activities that shape your thought life.

5. Accountability Partnership: Find a trusted friend or mentor who can help you identify blind spots in your thinking and encourage you in the renewal process.

The Role of the Holy Spirit

While we actively participate in renewing our minds, we must remember that true transformation comes through the power of the Holy Spirit. He illuminates Scripture, reveals truth, and provides the strength we need to maintain new thought patterns. Regular prayer for His guidance and empowerment should accompany our efforts at mental renewal.

Overcoming Common Challenges

Many people struggle with two major challenges in this process: consistency and resistance to change. To maintain consistency, start with small, manageable commitments rather than attempting dramatic changes all at once. When facing resistance, remember that discomfort often accompanies growth. View it as a sign that actual change is occurring.

Measuring Progress

There are several signs that show progress in mind renewal:
   - Increased peace and emotional stability
   - Greater resilience in facing challenges
   - More consistent alignment between beliefs and actions
   - Improved ability to recognize and reject false thinking
   - Increasing ability to use biblical principles in everyday life

Remember that renewing the mind is not a onetime event, but a lifelong process. Each day presents new opportunities to choose truth over falsehood, to align our thinking with God's Word, and to experience the transformation that comes through renewed thinking. As we persist in this process, we gradually experience the freedom and fulfillment that comes from having our minds transformed by truth.

The journey of mind renewal requires patience, persistence, and grace. Celebrate progress while maintaining a commitment to continued growth. Through consistent practice and reliance on the Holy Spirit, we can experience the profound transformation that begins with the renewal of our minds.

Biblical Meditation: A Key to Transformation

We've talked about the importance of renewing our minds, but how do we make it part of our daily lives? The answer is found in an ancient practice that God Himself gave us—biblical meditation.

When Joshua was preparing to lead the people of Israel, God gave him a powerful instruction: "Keep this Book of the Law always on your lips; meditate on it day and night, so that you may be careful to do everything written in it. Then you will be prosperous and successful" (Joshua 1:8, NIV). This shows us that meditating on God's Word is the key to not just knowing the truth, but living it.

Think of mind renewal as preparing the soil of our hearts, while biblical meditation is the act of planting and nurturing the seeds of truth that will eventually bear fruit in our lives. Just as a garden requires consistent attention and care, our minds need regular, focused engagement with God's Word to experience lasting transformation.

In the upcoming chapter, **The Battle of the Mind...**" we will explore the daily struggle of renewing our minds. Understanding how to identify the enemy and develop strategies to overcome these challenges is essential for maintaining our spiritual and emotional well-being.

CHAPTER 14

THE BATTLE OF THE MIND: ANXIETY, DEPRESSION, AND STRESS

In the previous chapter, we focused on "Renewing the Mind: The Foundation of Transformation," emphasizing how our thoughts shape our spiritual growth and daily life. We saw that scriptural renewal is the first step in aligning ourselves with God's truth instead of conforming to worldly patterns. Building on that foundation, this chapter delves into three primary challenges—anxiety, depression, and stress—that often undermine our pursuit of transformation. As we examine these struggles, we will see how a biblically renewed mind, supported by practical, research-based strategies, can help us experience the peace and wholeness Christ promises.

The Reality of Mental Battles

Have you ever thought about how much your heart affects every part of your life? Proverbs 4:23 says, "Keep your heart with all diligence, for out of it spring the issues of life." This verse powerfully reminds us that our inner world—the thoughts and feelings in our hearts and minds—is a battlefield. The enemy continually tries to plant seeds of doubt, fear, and condemnation there.

Proverbs 23:7 also offers great insight: "As a man thinks, so is he." In other words, our primary thoughts guide the direction of our lives. What we choose to focus on each day shapes our attitudes, emotions, and decisions. Think about how different your life could look if your daily thoughts were filled with faith-driven, positive ideas.

The challenge arises when God's Word is shared and takes root in our hearts. As described in Mark 4:15, Satan comes immediately to steal that Word—using distractions and negative thoughts to weaken our faith and rob us of peace. Meanwhile, Jesus promises His followers a life marked by peace: "My peace I give to you..." (John 14:27). Scripture also warns that the enemy, Satan, seeks to sow fear and confusion in our minds to keep us from experiencing this peace.

The key to winning the battle for your mind is to first identify the enemy, understand how he attacks, and learn how to defeat him. Thankfully, Scripture gives us all we need to recognize his tactics and stand firm in victory. God has not left us unequipped in this fight. Through His Word, we gain the wisdom, strength, and guidance necessary to overcome the enemy's lies and distractions. Once we understand who our adversary is (the devil), we can begin discerning how he attacks. And by recognizing his methods, we will stand in victory—just as Jesus did when tempted by Satan, responding to every challenge with the Word of God.

The Battle Against The Mind: Anxiety, Depression, & Stress 'ADS'

Jesus says in Matthew 6:31, "Therefore take no thought, saying, 'What shall we eat?' or 'What shall we drink?' or 'Wherewithal shall we be clothed?'" Notice how Jesus teaches us not to "take" worrisome thoughts by voicing them out loud. While we can't always control the thoughts that enter our minds, we do control how we respond. We don't have to accept or receive those thoughts, and we certainly shouldn't give them life by speaking them. As Proverbs 18:21 tells us, "Death and life are in the power of the tongue."

Our words grant permission for certain influences to operate in our lives, so be intentional about what you speak. When we voice negative, fearful, or anxious thoughts, we empower them. That is exactly why the devil seeks to manipulate us into giving voice to our anxieties and fears.

The three primary mental assaults Satan often uses to rob believers of God's peace are anxiety, depression, and stress—"ADS." These tactics can stir our emotions and prompt us to speak in agreement with them. Yet if we refuse to give voice to these thoughts and instead declare God's truth, we remove their power and stand firm in the victory Christ has won for us.

Spiritual Foundations: The Heart and the Mind

1. Out of the Heart Flow, the Issues of Life
Proverbs 4:23 instructs, "Keep your heart with all diligence, for out of it spring the issues of life." Our heart and mind are the battlefield on which the enemy wants to sow doubt, fear, and condemnation. We must guard our hearts by protecting them from harmful influences.

2. As a Man Thinks, So Does He Become
Proverbs 23:7 tells us our lives move in the direction of our dominant thoughts. What we meditate on daily shapes our attitudes, emotions, and choices.

3. The Enemy's Strategy
When the Word is preached and sown into the heart, Satan comes immediately to steal it (Mark 4:15). He uses distractions and negative thoughts to erode our faith and peace.

Anxiety: Fear of the Future

Anxiety often grows from "what if" thoughts, such as "What if I lose my job?" Or what if this or that doesn't work?" "What if my relationship fails?" These worries fixate on possible future problems, creating panic and ongoing stress in the present. Constantly dwelling on worst-case scenarios hinders decision-making and erodes confidence.

Biblical Remedy

- **Philippians 4:6–7**: "Be anxious for nothing, but in everything by prayer and supplication, with thanksgiving, let your requests be made known to God..." This passage shows that prayerful dependence on God and a grateful heart immediately counteracts anxiety.

- **1 Peter 5:7**: "Casting all your care upon Him, for He cares for you." Here, Scripture points to a conscious act of handing our anxieties over to God, freeing us from fear.

Practical Application

1. Identify the source of your anxiety and surrender it to God in prayer.

2. Replace "what if" thinking with affirmations of faith, trusting in God's sovereignty.

Depression: Weight of the Past

Depression often stems from unresolved past hurts, regrets, guilt, or shame. Unprocessed emotional wounds can resurface, reinforcing negative thoughts and undermining a hopeful outlook. Over time, these burdens interfere with daily life, relationships, and well-being.

Biblical Remedy

- **Isaiah 61:3**: God promises to give "the garment of praise for the spirit of heaviness." Switching our focus from past wounds to God's faithfulness transforms the atmosphere of our hearts.

- **Psalm 34:18**: "The LORD is near to those who have a broken heart..." God's nearness provides comfort and healing.

Practical Application

1. Practice forgiveness—both toward yourself and others—to release the past's painful hold.

2. Meditate on Scriptures that emphasize God's grace and ability to restore.

Understanding Stress and Pressure

Stress is often the response we feel when too much is happening at once. It can lead to worry, fatigue, and even anxiety. But viewing stress as "pressure" can shift how we handle it.

Pressure can be managed, like adjusting the water flow in a hose. Too much pressure can cause damage, but when controlled, it's manageable. Similarly, recognizing stress as pressure reminds us it can be regulated.

Scripture reveals we are built to handle a certain level of pressure. The real struggle begins when we let our feelings, rather than God's promises, dictate our perception of what we can handle.

Biblical Remedy

- **1 Corinthians 10:13**: God will not allow us to be tempted (or pressured) beyond what we can bear.

- **Isaiah 26:3**: "You will keep him in perfect peace, whose mind is stayed on You, because he trusts in You." Steadfast trust in God keeps our minds anchored in peace.

Practical Application

1. Develop healthy routines (rest, exercise, prayer, fellowship).

2. Learn to say "no" when necessary to keep responsibilities in balance and maintain peace.

The Power of Renewing the Mind

As discussed in the previous chapter, renewing our minds is essential for victory over mental battles (Romans 12:2).

1. **Taking Thoughts Captive**

   ○ **2 Corinthians 10:5**: We demolish arguments and every pretension raised against the knowledge of God by taking every thought captive. This active engagement—challenging negative self-talk and replacing it with scriptural truth—builds an environment of faith.

2. **Standing Firm Against the Enemy**

   ○ **2 Timothy 1:7**: "God has not given us a spirit of fear, but of power and of love and of a sound mind." Recognize and reject the spirit of fear, and invite the Spirit of peace through prayer, worship, and obedience.

As we stand firm on God's Word, we realize we can face life's challenges with confidence. When we rely on the truth of Scripture, we overcome the mental attacks of anxiety, depression, and stress. However, the question remains: *How do we sustain this empowered mindset day after day?* The answer lies in deepening our relationship with God through biblical meditation.

Next Step: Biblical Meditation

In the next chapter, we will explore how meditating on Scripture can transform our thoughts and strengthen our ability to handle pressure. By immersing ourselves in God's Word, we discover peace, guidance, and renewed strength to face life's challenges with faith and assurance. Let us now take the next step and discover the powerful practice of biblical meditation.

CHAPTER 15

BIBLICAL MEDITATION

As we discussed in the previous chapter, renewing your mind is a powerful and life-changing process, but it's not something that happens on its own. Identifying unhealthy thought patterns and replacing them with God's truth lays the foundation for transformation. But how do we make these truths stick? How do we move from simply knowing God's Word to living it out every day?

In a world filled with noise and distractions, finding a moment of peace can feel impossible. Yet, the Bible invites us into a practice that not only calms our hearts but also transforms our minds—meditation. Unlike worldly meditation, which often focuses on emptying the mind, biblical meditation fills your mind with the truth of God's Word, allowing His voice to shape your thoughts, decisions, and identity.

This is where biblical meditation becomes the bridge that connects the renewal of our minds to real-life application. It's more than simply reading Scripture; it's about deeply reflecting on God's promises and letting them take root in your heart. Just as a gardener waters and nurtures newly planted seeds, biblical meditation helps the truth of God's Word grow into lasting transformation.

In this chapter, we'll uncover what it means to meditate on God's Word, why it's essential for spiritual growth, and how this powerful practice can draw you closer to God while equipping you to live out His purpose for your life.

Biblical Meditation: Aligning Your Mind with God's Word

"Blessed is the man who does not walk in the counsel of the wicked, nor stand in the way of sinners, nor sit in the seat of scoffers; but his delight is in the law of the Lord, and on His law, he meditates day and night. He is like a tree planted by streams of water that yields its fruit in its season, and its leaf does not wither. In all that he does, he prospers." — Psalm 1:1-3 (ESV).

Many Christians find the concept of meditation confusing. Let's explore what it means to meditate as followers of Jesus. We'll start by looking at the differences between Christian meditation and other forms.

The Bible frequently speaks about meditation. In Psalm 1:2, we read 'On His law, he meditates day and night.' The Psalmist declares, 'I will meditate on Your precepts and fix my eyes on Your ways' (Psalm 119:15), and prays 'May my meditation be pleasing to Him' (Psalm 104:34). These verses point to a specific focus: meditating on God's laws, precepts, ways, and truth.

This biblical approach stands in stark contrast to many Eastern or New Age practices, where meditation is about emptying the mind, stopping the flow of thoughts, and 'quieting the heart.'

As Christians, our goal is different - we seek to fill our minds and hearts with God's Word and His presence. Rather than emptying ourselves, we open ourselves to be filled and shaped by the Holy Spirit through God's Word.

Understanding Biblical Meditation

Biblical meditation means reflecting, contemplating, and deeply considering who God is and what He has communicated in His Word. We meditate on Scripture by reading it slowly, breaking it down phrase by phrase, praying through its meaning, and asking how it applies to our lives. The goal is to process God's truth, allowing it to permeate our thinking practically. Memorizing Scripture can also facilitate meditation, as we recall verses throughout the day, considering their meaning and application.

This practice of immersing our minds in God's truth renews our thinking and transforms us to be more like Jesus (Romans 12:2). Regular biblical meditation helps guard our hearts and nourish our souls daily. It keeps us rooted in truth amid competing voices and strengthens our faith as we remember God's past faithfulness and promises for the future.

HOW TO MEDITATE ON GOD'S WORD

Biblical meditation is simple, but it does take focus and commitment. Here's a step-by-step guide to help you get started:

1. Pick a Scripture Verse or Passage.

    Choose a short verse or passage from the Bible that's meaningful to you, perhaps a promise from God or a verse that speaks to a current challenge.

2. Read It Slowly

    Take time with the verse, reading it several times and letting the words sink in. Reading aloud can help you focus and absorb the meaning more deeply.

3. Think About the Word Examine: keywords and phrases carefully,

asking yourself:

- What is God saying in this passage?

- How does this apply to my life right now?

- What does this teach me about God's character?

1. Pray About What You've Read
   Transform the Scripture into prayer. Thank God for His Word, seek wisdom to understand it, and ask for guidance in living it out.

2. Write Down Your Thoughts
   Keep a journal to record what you're learning. This practice helps cement the lessons and provides a record of your spiritual journey.

3. Think About the Verse Throughout the Day
   Memorize the verse or keep it accessible for reflection throughout your day, allowing it to guide your thoughts and actions.

Daily Meditation Practices

Like any spiritual discipline, biblical meditation grows stronger with consistent practice. To develop this habit:

- Set aside a specific time each day, whether morning, lunch break, or evening

- Create a peaceful space free from distractions

- Use tools like devotional books, Bible apps, or worship music to enhance focus

- Stay flexible and gentle with yourself when life interrupts your routine

Managing Distractions

Distractions are one of the biggest challenges in meditation. Here are some practical ways to stay focused:

- To maintain focus during meditation:

- Set clear boundaries by turning off your phone or finding a quiet space

- Start with short five-minute sessions and gradually increase duration

- Keep a notepad nearby to jot down distracting thoughts

Biblical Meditation Transformative Impact

When you make biblical meditation a regular part of your life, you'll begin to see its impact in many areas:

1. Regular biblical meditation brings profound benefits:

2. Strengthens relationships through the application of biblical principles

3. Enhances decision-making with divine wisdom

4. Helps overcome fear and anxiety through trust in God's promises

5. Deepens your spiritual growth and relationship with God

Uncovering Internal Flaws or Issues

Through meditation, the Holy Spirit gently reveals areas needing transformation. As Psalm 139:23-24 reminds us: 'Search me, God, and know my heart; test me and know my anxious thoughts. See if there is any offensive way in me, and lead me in the way everlasting.'

This revelation process:

- Brings awareness of negative thought patterns and unhealthy habits

- Opens doors for God's transformative power

- Prepares us for deeper change

The upcoming chapter will explore how to identify and rewrite these default patterns through God's wisdom and grace.

CHAPTER 16

EXPLORING OUR DEFAULT PATTERNS

Each of us has habits and beliefs that influence our thoughts, emotions, and actions—frequently without our awareness. We refer to these as default patterns, similar to autopilot behaviors that guide us through life, even when we are not consciously in control.

Default Patterns: *The Invisible Scripts Guiding Our Lives*

Psychologists refer to "default patterns" or "default modes" as automatic, habitual, and often unconscious ways of thinking, feeling, and behaving. These patterns are shaped by past experiences, learning, and environments, and can influence our perceptions, emotions, and actions.

The Four Types of Default Patterns

1. Cognitive Biases / How We Think

Our natural thought patterns can sometimes lead us astray, influencing our perception of reality in ways we may not fully understand. For example, we might only notice things that confirm what we already believe, a phenomenon known as confirmation bias, which can prevent us from seeing the bigger picture or considering alternative viewpoints.

Additionally, we may focus too much on the negative while ignoring the positive, a tendency referred to as negativity bias, which can distort our overall outlook on life. These cognitive biases shape our decision-making processes and can have significant implications for our relationships and mental well-being, often leading us to miss out on valuable opportunities for growth and connection. Recognizing these biases in ourselves is a crucial step toward cultivating a more balanced and open-minded perspective.

2. Emotional Reactivity / How We Feel

The way we're wired can also influence our emotions. It might make us quicker to feel anxious, angry, or overwhelmed, even when the situation doesn't call for it.

3. Behavioral Habits / What We Do

Our habits often come from these default patterns, like putting off important tasks (procrastination) or turning to unhealthy ways to cope with stress.

4. Relationship Patterns / How We Relate to Others

The way we connect with people is shaped by these patterns, too. They affect how we form attachments, communicate, and handle conflicts in our relationships.

Although we might not be aware of them, default patterns have a considerable influence on our lives and relationships. These patterns come from our core beliefs and automatic emotional reactions—things we often overlook in the rush of daily life.

Take, for instance, someone who's overly self-critical. Without even noticing, they might make negative comments about themselves or dwell on self-defeating thoughts. This inner dialogue can quietly chip away at their confidence and influence how they connect with others.

When we take time to examine these hidden patterns, we start to understand why we act the way we do—and that awareness is the key to change.

It's like turning on a light to reveal the unseen scripts guiding our behavior. By examining these unconscious default patterns, we can understand why we behave a certain way and make necessary changes. It's like shining a light on the invisible scripts running through our minds.

Recognizing these patterns is the first step toward breaking habits that don't serve us. By replacing them with healthier ones, we can build stronger relationships and improve our overall well-being.

Maladaptive Patterns

Maladaptive patterns are unhealthy ways of responding to situations or environments. They often start as protective mechanisms, helping us cope with challenging circumstances. However, over time, these patterns can turn into harmful habits that shape how we see and interact with the world.

Example of a Maladaptive Pattern:

"People Pleasing": One common example of a maladaptive pattern is **people-pleasing behavior.** This pattern involves constantly prioritizing others' needs over one's own to gain approval or avoid conflict. While it may seem helpful or selfless on the surface, it often leads to negative outcomes, such as burnout, resentment, and a diminished sense of self-worth.

Dysfunctional Patterns

Dysfunctional patterns go a step further. They include thoughts, emotions, or behaviors that interfere with our daily lives, strain relationships, or block us from reaching our goals.

Some default patterns develop as a way to protect us, especially if we've experienced trauma or abuse. These are often called "maladaptive" or "dysfunctional" patterns, and while they may have helped us cope in the past, they can hold us back in the present.

Common Dysfunctional Behavior Patterns

1. **Avoidance Patterns:**

   Individuals may actively avoid situations or emotions that remind them of a traumatic experience in an effort to minimize distress.

   - **Example:** After a painful divorce, Anna avoids social gatherings at church because she fears hearing conversations about marriage or seeing couples, which might stir painful memories. Instead, she isolates herself to protect her emotions.

   - **Comment:** Anna's avoidance is her way of self-preservation. Approaching her with Christ-like compassion—offering understanding, comfort, and a listening ear—can gently support her healing process. Encouraging her to trust in God's restorative love can help her take steps toward reengaging with her community.

2. **Hyper-vigilance Patterns:** Hyper-vigilant individuals are constantly on high alert for potential threats, often driven by a deep distrust of others as a means of self-protection.

   - **Example:** After the emotional trauma of a failed business venture, Malcolm becomes excessively cautious and distrustful of new business partners. His hyper-focus on every detail prevents him from experiencing peace.

- ○ Comment: Malcolm's hyper-vigilance is rooted in the pain of past failures. Encouraging him to trust God's plan and seek divine wisdom can help him rebuild trust, discerning relationships with faith and confidence.

3. **Emotional Numbing Patterns:**
This involves suppressing or disconnecting from emotions to cope with overwhelming pain associated with trauma.

- ○ **Example:** After enduring years of emotional abuse, Mia has learned to suppress her feelings. She detaches herself and avoids emotional pain by shutting down entirely.

- ○ **Comment:** Mia's emotional numbing is a self-protective response to deep wounds. Gently reminding her that God sees her pain, understands her struggles, and loves her deeply can offer hope and strength. With time and assurance of His care, she can begin to heal and reconnect with her emotions.

4. **Self-Sabotaging Patterns:** Some individuals engage in behaviors that block their success, often as a way to punish themselves or remain in a victim mindset.

- ○ **Example:** James, who has experienced multiple failed relationships, pushes away potential romantic partners out of fear of more heartbreak, reinforcing a cycle of loneliness.

- ○ **Comment:** After experiencing several failed relationships, James pushes away new romantic partners, fearing another heartbreak. This creates a self-perpetuating cycle of loneliness.

5. **Approval-Seeking Patterns:** An excessive need for validation often leads to people-pleasing, rooted in low self-esteem from past emotional wounds.

   ○ **Example:** After traumatic experiences at work, Rachel constantly seeks validation from her colleagues, believing her value depends on their approval.

   ○ **Comment:** Rachel's approval-seeking stems from a deep need for affirmation. Helping her understand that her worth comes from Christ's unconditional love can build her self-confidence and provide lasting peace.

Breaking Free From Dysfunctional Patterns

Many maladaptive and dysfunctional patterns originate from deep psychological wounds—painful experiences that shape how we think, feel, and behave. These wounds leave a lasting imprint, often influencing our actions in ways we may not even recognize. The first crucial step toward healing and personal growth is identifying and understanding these patterns.

While these maladaptive behaviors often begin as coping mechanisms to help us survive difficult circumstances, over time, they can become deeply ingrained. Left unchecked, they continue to feed unhealthy thoughts, emotions, and actions that keep us stuck and prevent true healing.

The good news is that it is entirely possible to break free from these cycles. With God's healing power and guidance, the mind, heart, and spirit can be restored, paving the way for a life filled with freedom, growth, and renewal.

Let me share a real-life story about a woman who, through the transformative power of God's love, overcame destructive patterns rooted in past trauma and stepped into a life of hope and wholeness.

Mary's Story: Overcoming Destructive Default Patterns

Years ago, I met Mary (a pseudonym) during one of the most challenging seasons of her life. She appeared worn out, emotionally drained, and weighed down by yet another failed relationship. As we began counseling, Mary shared her heartbreak and confusion, expressing frustration over feeling stuck in a repeating cycle of failed love.

As I listened, I understood that Mary's struggles stemmed from her deeply rooted, negative unconscious patterns. My role as her counselor became clear: to help her uncover and confront these hidden influences. I encouraged her to create a relationship timeline, documenting the emotional highs and lows, the traits she sought in partners, and the recurring conflicts she experienced.

What emerged was a striking revelation. Mary's fear of rejection caused her to emotionally withdraw as her relationships grew deeper. Sometimes, she would push her partners away intentionally, but often it was unintentional—an automatic response she didn't fully understand. As we dug deeper, Mary revealed a painful truth: she had endured abuse as a child. This trauma shaped her protective behaviors and distorted her perception of love.

Instead of the nurturing love she needed as a child, she suffered abuse, leading her to develop a distorted belief that love and pain are inseparable. Though loving guardians eventually rescued her from that abusive home, Mary struggled to fully accept their care and affection. Her childhood wounds had planted a lie deep within her heart—that she was unworthy of love. This belief, left unchallenged, continued to sabotage her relationships well into adulthood.

One day, during our session, I gently brought this to her attention. "Mary," I said, "deep down, it seems you struggle to embrace love because you don't believe you deserve it. This belief not only shapes your relationships with others, but also affects your connection with God."

Her reaction was immediate and intense. Anger flickered in her eyes, and I braced myself for the possibility that she might walk out, as others had when faced with hard truths. Instead, Mary turned her chair toward the window, her body rigid with tension. For a long moment, she sat in silence, staring into the distance. Then, with a voice barely above a whisper, she said, "Please continue."

The Window Moment

In that moment, I saw both Mary's deep pain and her fragile readiness for change. Though she remained fiercely guarded, her wounded heart was yearning for the healing it desperately needed.

I paused, silently praying for wisdom and strength to guide her through this pivotal moment. As Mary continued gazing out the window, her face softened, and a faint smile emerged. Curious, I leaned forward to see what had captured her attention. Outside, a father was playfully tossing his two young children one at a time into the air as they squealed with delight, begging him to "do it again."

Mary's smile widened, and I could sense the little girl within her—the one who had been robbed of such innocent joy—experiencing a bittersweet moment of connection. I also felt God's Fatherly heart longing to pour out His love for Mary far greater than what she was witnessing.

When she turned back to me, her smile was gone, replaced by a somber expression. "I want to believe that God is different," she said softly. "I want to believe He could love me unconditionally. But how can I trust that? How can I believe in a loving father when the only example I've ever had was so... evil?" Her voice wavered, and tears filled her eyes.

I leaned forward, speaking gently yet firm. "Mary, God's love is nothing like your earthly father's. His love is pure, constant, and unchanging. He loves you so much that He gave His Son to die for you. That's how much you matter to Him—not for what you do, but for who you are."

Mary's eyes met mine, filled with a mixture of pain and doubt. Then suddenly, her emotions erupted in anger. She stood abruptly and shouted, "Then why would He let those horrible things happen to me? Where was God's love when my mother abandoned me? Where was His love when my father, when he... when he, did those awful things to me? Things no father should ever do to his..." Her voice trailed off, breaking under the weight of unspoken words.

Mary turned away, trembling as she fought to hold back tears. I remained silent, offering her unspoken support through my quiet, empathetic presence. I understood she needed this moment to release the anger and face the pain she had buried for so long. To speak too soon would have been to interrupt the healing process.

So, I waited, patient and prayerful, knowing that in time Mary would not only ask the hard questions but would also be ready to hear the answers that would lead her toward healing.

Raw Emotions Unleashed

As Mary paced the room, her emotions erupted like a storm—anger, pain, and desperation pouring out in a torrent. "Why didn't God stop it? Why didn't He protect me? If He loved me, why did He allow all those horrible things to happen?" she cried, her voice cracking under the weight of her anguish.

Then Mary's tone shifted. It softened, trembling with the fragile innocence of the little girl she had been. Her words, barely above a whisper, were filled with unimaginable pain. "Things no father should ever do... to his daughter, to his little girl?" The words lingered in the air, carrying decades of suppressed sorrow and unanswered questions that had haunted her for so long.

I saw the war within Mary—a mix of relief at finally voicing the unspeakable and disgust at the memories now laid bare. Yet, in releasing her buried emotions, Mary also reclaimed a part of herself. It was as if the act of speaking those words began to loosen the chains she had carried for over 20 years. For the first time, a faint glimmer of hope broke through the darkness, hinting at the possibility of healing and freedom.

The room fell silent, the weight of Mary's raw pain and fragile hope lingering in the air. Slowly, I stood and moved closer, meeting her tear-filled eyes with deep compassion. "Mary," I began gently, "God's heart broke for you during those terrible moments. He didn't want those things to happen. What you endured wasn't His will—it was the result of sinful, evil choices made by a person misusing their free will. God hates that kind of evil, and He promises justice. He will hold accountable those who caused you such harm, including your mother, for abandoning you."

I let the truth of those words sink in before continuing. "But Mary, please hear this: God has always loved you. Even in your darkest moments, even when you felt too broken to cry out to Him, He was there. He never left you, and He's here now, ready to heal your deepest wounds—if you'll let Him."

Mary stood motionless, her arms crossed tightly over her chest as though shielding herself from further hurt. Her expression was a mixture of longing and fear. Finally, in a voice barely audible, she whispered, "I want to believe that. I really do. But I don't know how."

Mary's words were both a confession and a plea—a tentative step toward the healing she so desperately wanted but didn't yet know how to embrace. I recognized this as the start of her journey, a pivotal moment where everything hinged on what I would say next. Silently, I prayed for God's wisdom to guide my words and help her move forward.

Breakthrough And Restoration

"The thing about love, Mary," I continued softly, "is that it must be freely given and freely received, or it ceases to be love at all. Despite all the terrible things your father did to you as a little girl, you still longed to give him your love. But as you shared with me, your father not only rejected you but also the love you tried to offer him. That rejection, you said, hurt just as deeply as the evil he committed against you."

Mary groaned audibly, turning away to face the window. Her face twisted in pain as though she were reliving those moments of rejection. "Mary," I said softly, "God is offering you His unconditional love and healing. You don't need to earn His love or prove your worth—His love for you has always been, and always will be, unchanging and unconditional."

I paused before asking, "Mary, will you reject God's love the way your father rejected yours? You know how deeply that rejection wounded you. Now, imagine how much more it pains the heart of God, who is love itself, when His love is rejected by you.

Mary turned from the window, her eyes locking onto mine. At first, her expression was one of pain, a visible acknowledgment of the truth she could no longer deny. She realized she had been projecting her father's rejection of her onto God, pushing Him away just as she had pushed others away in an attempt to shield herself from more pain.

Then something shifted. The truth—that God loved her completely, without judgment or conditions—began to sink in. A faint smile appeared on her face, and her eyes filled with the wide-eyed wonder of a child hearing the best news imaginable. Those words pierced through the walls of pain, anger, and fear that had held her captive for so long.

I watched as doubt transformed into hope. This hope opened the door of Mary's heart, enabling her finally to receive God's love. Tears streamed down her face as she stepped toward me and embraced me, sobbing like a child seeking the safety of her father's arms. Mary released years of pent-up anger, shame, and pain in that embrace. In that moment, she let go of the lies that had imprisoned her for so long and allowed God's healing love to fill her soul.

I led Mary in a heartfelt prayer as she recommitted her life to Christ, inviting Him into her deepest and most wounded places. It was a sacred moment—one in which Mary chose to surrender, believe in God's love, and trust in His healing power.

In the months that followed, Mary courageously continued her journey of healing. Through scripture, prayer, and counseling, she faced her pain head-on, replacing the destructive patterns of her past with the truth of God's Word. She forgave her abuser, relinquishing the bitterness and shame that had weighed her down for so many years.

Over a year and a half later, I had the honor of witnessing the fruits of Mary's transformation. She walked down the aisle to marry a godly man who cherished and valued her for who she was. The radiant joy on her face was undeniable—a living testimony to the healing and transformative power of God's love.

Insights Gained from Mary's Journey

Mary's story is a powerful reminder that no wound is too deep for God to heal. When we surrender our brokenness to Him, He can transform our lives, restore our hearts, and replace destructive patterns with His truth. If you, like Mary, feel trapped by pain, shame, or the fear of rejection, know this: God sees you. He knows your struggles and loves you unconditionally. God's love isn't something you have to earn—it's freely given. His grace is enough to heal every wound and break every chain that holds you captive.

Listen, you no longer need to carry the weight of your past. The walls you've built to protect yourself may now be blocking the healing and freedom you desire. Surrender those walls to God and allow His love to reach the deepest parts of your heart. Let Him replace the lies you've believed with His truth: that you are cherished, valued, and worthy of love.

A Prayer for Healing and Freedom

Heavenly Father,

I come to You with my pain and fears, surrendering my burdens. Thank You for Your unconditional love. Heal my wounds and replace lies with Your truth. Fill my heart with peace and transform me. I invite You into my life; lead me to healing and community. In Jesus Name; Amen.

In the next chapter, we'll explore practical, Bible-based strategies for 'breaking negative behavior patterns.' Together, we'll uncover how God's Word, the guidance of the Holy Spirit, and intentional actions can work to set us free. Through this process, we can move toward a life of renewed purpose, joy, and peace.

CHAPTER 17

HOW TO BREAK NEGATIVE BEHAVIOR PATTERNS

We have uncovered the presence of default patterns—hidden scripts that subtly shape our lives. Each of us carries habits and beliefs that influence our thoughts, emotions, and actions, often without us even realizing it. These internalized norms and routines become so ingrained that they can dictate our behavior in various situations, often leading us to react automatically.

These default patterns function much like autopilot behaviors, steering us through life when we are not consciously aware or in control. They silently guide our responses, shaping our decisions and interactions in ways we may not immediately recognize.

Understanding these patterns can offer us profound insights into our behaviors and motivations, paving the way for personal growth. By bringing awareness to these hidden influences, we can begin to challenge and change them, leading to more intentional and fulfilling lives.

Ultimately, recognizing and addressing our default scripts can transform the way we interact with ourselves and the world around us.

By the grace of God, through counseling, and the power of the Holy Spirit, Mary was able to recognize and break free from the negative patterns that had ensnared her. Once we identify the root causes of our bad habits, we can begin the process of change.

Breaking established habits is one of the toughest challenges we face because the neural pathways that support those habits become deeply ingrained in our brains through years of repetition. It requires prayer, ongoing effort, and a strong dedication to disrupt the cycle and create new, positive routines.

If friends or family members enable your unhealthy behaviors, it may be necessary to limit your time with them or establish boundaries. Our social circles exert a significant influence on our thoughts and actions.

When we are surrounded by individuals who exhibit and reinforce negative tendencies, overcoming those same flaws within ourselves becomes increasingly challenging. Occasionally, creating physical and emotional distance from toxic influences becomes essential for personal growth.

If specific environments or situations tend to lead us toward sin or provoke regression into destructive patterns, it's imperative to distance ourselves from such influences.

Even stimuli we may not consciously notice can reactivate old neural pathways and contribute to harmful habits before we become aware of what's happening.

By proactively identifying and eliminating these triggers, you can prevent many negative patterns from developing. Common triggers often include stressful situations, certain locations, specific smells, or interactions with particular people.

Self-awareness, self-control, and conscious choices are key to breaking free from our usual negative patterns. We have to uproot the habits at their core by becoming aware of our default behaviors and what internal motivations drive them.

Relying on God's strength instead of just our own willpower, and consciously surrendering to Christ's guidance moment by moment, is essential for overcoming harmful patterns. Human effort alone is insufficient to break free from habitual sin. True transformation in our lives can only occur when we remain steadfast in Christ.

The Corruption of the Fallen World

Romans 12:2; "And be not conformed to this world: but be ye transformed by the renewing of your mind..." The fallen world has corrupted the human mind, leading to harmful thought patterns and behaviors.

Scripture warns us not to conform to the corrupt systems of the world but instead to allow our minds to be renewed and transformed by the Holy Spirit through the Word of God.

If the influences of the world have impacted our thoughts, the encouraging news is that we can renew our minds and find freedom through repentance and the transforming work of the Holy Spirit within us. As Ezekiel 36:26 promises, "I will give you a new heart and put a new spirit in you; I will remove from you your heart of stone and give you a heart of flesh."

How to Break Free

As Mary's story illustrated, relying on God, understanding our weaknesses, and committing to improving our choices each day are crucial. She sought and received healing and deliverance from the destructive patterns she had become a victim of. Through the power of God's love and her willingness to face the pain of her past, Mary found freedom and restoration.

By addressing the wounds that had once defined her, Mary not only broke free from the cycles of dysfunction but also discovered a new sense of purpose and joy in her life. Her journey reminds us that no matter how deeply ingrained these patterns may be, they can be overcome when we partner with God.

We, too, can break negative and destructive patterns. Whether rooted in past trauma, unhealthy relationships, or distorted self-beliefs, these patterns don't have to define our future. With the right strategies and persistence, anyone can break free from the negative cycles holding them back and cultivate healthier ways of thinking and behaving. And replace them with healthy, life-affirming habits that reflect God's truth and purpose for us.

The next personal issue we need to tackle is just as important as the current one. In fact, if you don't address both issues, you won't be able to resolve either of them.

Negative Self-Talk: Confronting Your Inner Critic

Breaking negative behavior patterns is an important part of growing as a person and in your faith. As we have learned, these patterns are often rooted in past hurts, unhealthy relationships, or false beliefs about yourself.

The good news is, they don't have to control your future. By using the right strategies and staying committed, you can let go of harmful habits and replace them with healthy ones that reflect God's truth and purpose for your life.

To remain free from negative behavior patterns, we need to avoid reinforcing them with negative self-talk. Therefore, it is important that you focus on the source of many of these struggles: your inner voice. That constant stream of self-talk, whether encouraging or critical, has the power to shape your decisions, influence your emotions, and reinforce the habits you're trying to change.

Negative self-talk affects every area of your life. By learning to align your thoughts with God's Word, you can not only break free from destructive cycles, but also create a mindset that helps you grow and thrive. Let's study the impact of your thoughts and learn how to infuse positivity into every aspect of your journey.

Breaking Free from Negative Self-Talk

Have you noticed how that little voice in your head can sometimes be your harshest critic? As Christians, we are called to spread hope and God's love to others. But here's something often overlooked: sometimes the most important person we need to show love and grace to is ourselves.

This journey of breaking free from negative self-talk is about aligning your thoughts with God's truth, recognizing His voice within, and living in the fullness of who He created you to be.

The Battle Within

Think about your day yesterday. Did you catch yourself thinking or saying things like "I can't do this," "I'm not good enough," or "Why do I even bother?" Many of us engage in this kind of self-talk without even realizing it.

Often, we are harder on ourselves than we would ever dream of being on a loved one. But is this how God wants us to treat ourselves—the masterpiece He created in His own image?

In Matthew 12:36-37, Jesus reminds us of the power of words: *"But I tell you that everyone will have to give account on the day of judgment for every empty word they have spoken. For by your words you will be acquitted, and by your words, you will be condemned."*

This truth doesn't just apply to the words we speak to others, but also to the words we speak to ourselves. Negative self-talk isn't just a harmless habit; it's agreement with lies that contradict God's Word about who we are.

Understanding Negative Self-Talk

Negative self-talk is like having an internal critic that magnifies your flaws and minimizes your strengths. Here are some common examples:

- **"I'll never be good enough."**

- **"Everyone else is better than me."**

- **"I always mess things up."**

- **"God probably doesn't even care about me."**

These thoughts feel powerful and convincing in the moment, but they're rooted in lies. God's Word offers a vastly different narrative about your identity and worth.

Common Sources of Negative Self-Talk

1. **Past Experiences:** Words spoken over us in childhood or past failures can leave deep wounds that resurface in self-criticism.

2. **Cultural Pressures:** Society often sets unattainable standards for success, beauty, or intelligence, leaving us feeling inadequate.

3. **Spiritual Warfare:** The enemy thrives on planting seeds of doubt, fear, and insecurity, hoping you'll forget God's truth.

The Real-World Impact

Negative self-talk doesn't just exist in your mind; it influences every aspect of your life:

1. Mental Health

Constant self-criticism is like a slow-dripping poison to your mind. It feeds anxiety, depression, and feelings of unworthiness. But Jesus offers peace and joy. *"Peace I leave with you; my peace, I give you. I do not give to you as the world gives. Do not let your hearts be troubled and do not be afraid"* (John 14:27). Negative self-talk blocks this peace, keeping you from experiencing the joy God intends for you.

2. Relationships

Negative self-talk can lead to destructive patterns in relationships. For instance:

- You might push others away, believing you're unworthy of love or connection.

- Alternatively, you might settle for unhealthy relationships, thinking you don't deserve better.

When we see ourselves through God's eyes, we can approach relationships with confidence and grace.

3. Dreams and Goals

Have you ever allowed a dream to die because of fear or self-doubt? It's a disheartening experience to look back and realize that we have let our aspirations slip away due to the internal battles we face. I acknowledge I have been guilty of that, and it serves as a reminder of the importance of courage and belief in oneself, even when the path seems uncertain. We often let the whispers of doubt cloud our judgment, preventing us from pursuing what truly brings us joy and fulfillment.

Perhaps you wanted to start a new career, pursue a ministry, or develop a talent, but that inner voice said, "You'll fail."

Negative self-talk can hold you back from stepping into the plans God has for you.

"For I know the plans I have for you," declares the Lord, "plans to prosper you and not to harm you, plans to give you hope and a future" (Jeremiah 29:11).

God's Truth vs. Our Self-Talk

When we believe lies about ourselves, we disagree with God's Word. Let's contrast common negative self-talk with God's truth:

"I'm worthless."

"You are fearfully and wonderfully made" (Psalm 139:14).

"I can't do this."

"I can do all things through Christ who strengthens me" (Philippians 4:13).

"Nobody loves me."

"I have loved you with an everlasting love" (Jeremiah 31:3).

"I always fail."

"In all these things we are more than conquerors through him who loved us" (Romans 8:37).

God's truth about you is unshakable, and when you align yourself-talk with His Word, you'll experience transformation.

Breaking Free: Actionable Steps

1. Catch Your Thoughts

The first step to change is awareness. Start paying attention to the things you say to yourself. Ask:

- Would I say this to a close friend?

- Does this thought align with God's Word?

For example, if you catch yourself thinking, "I'm such a failure," stop and reflect. Replace it with a truth like, "God uses my weaknesses to show His strength" (2 Corinthians 12:9).

2. Replace Lies with Truth

Negative thoughts won't simply disappear; you must actively replace them. **Take intentional steps to cultivate a positive mindset and strengthen your inner resilience.** Memorize Scriptures that speak to your worth and identity. Create a list of affirmations based on God's Word, such as:

- "I am loved unconditionally by God."

- "I am chosen and called for a purpose."

- "God is working all things together for my good."

3. Practice Gratitude

Gratitude is a powerful antidote to negativity, offering a transformative perspective on life. Each day, write down three things you're thankful for, no matter how small they may seem. By taking a moment to reflect on the positive aspects of your day, you can shift your focus away from challenges and cultivate a more optimistic mindset. This simple practice trains your mind to focus on blessings instead of shortcomings, ultimately enhancing your overall well-being and resilience against negative thoughts.

4. Pray for Renewal

Ask God to help you see yourself through His eyes. Romans 12:2 encourages us to be transformed by the renewal of our minds. Through prayer, God can replace your critical inner voice with His affirming presence.

5. Surround Yourself with Encouragement

Community matters. Share your journey with trusted friends, a mentor, or a Christian counselor. Their encouragement and perspective can remind you of God's truth when you struggle to see it.

Staying Free: Building New Habits

Breaking free from negative self-talk isn't a onetime event; it's a continual process of aligning your thoughts with God's truth. Here's how to maintain your freedom:

1. Regular Thought Checks

Make it a habit to evaluate your thoughts daily. Proverbs 4:23 warns, *"Above all else, guard your heart, for everything you do flows from it."* Keep your inner dialogue in check to prevent negativity from taking root.

2. Speak Life

Be intentional about speaking words of life over yourself and others. Proverbs 18:21 reminds us that the tongue holds the power of life and death. Use this power wisely.

3. Celebrate Progress

Acknowledge and celebrate the ways God is transforming your thoughts and attitudes, as this transformation is a profound work of grace in your life. Each moment of personal growth reflects His presence and guidance, reminding you of His endless love and faithfulness.

A Challenge for the Week

Take these actionable steps to start your journey:

1. **Thought Journal:** Write down negative thoughts as they arise. Next to each thought, record a corresponding truth from God's Word.

2. **Daily Affirmations:** Speak positive, Scripture-based affirmations over yourself each morning.

3. **Share with a Friend:** Discuss your progress with someone you trust. Their encouragement can strengthen your resolve.

A Prayer for Breaking Free

Heavenly Father, thank You for creating me in Your image and for loving me unconditionally. I confess that I have believed lies about myself, and I ask for Your help to replace these lies with Your truth. Renew my mind and fill me with thoughts that honor You. Help me to see myself as You see me—a beloved child with a purpose and a future. In Jesus' name, Amen.

Seeing Yourself Through God's Eyes

Breaking free from negative self-talk is about more than just improving your mood; it's about embracing the abundant life Jesus died to give you. When you see yourself through God's eyes, you'll realize that you are His masterpiece, equipped and empowered to live out His purpose for your life. Isn't it time to align your thoughts with the Creator who calls you beloved?

In the next chapter, we will explore the 'dangers of unhealed emotional trauma'—how it affects our lives, relationships, and spiritual growth. Understanding these consequences is key to breaking free from their hold and stepping into the abundant life God has promised. Through this exploration, we will uncover how to move from pain to healing, from bondage to freedom, and from despair to hope.

CHAPTER 18

THE DANGERS OF UNHEALED EMOTIONAL TRAUMA

As discussed in a previous chapter regarding Mary, experiencing a painful or traumatic event can leave significant emotional scars. If these traumatic wounds aren't addressed and healed appropriately, they can create a destructive cycle or pattern in an individual's life.

Unresolved Emotional Trauma

Unresolved emotional trauma leads to a cycle of negative thoughts, behaviors, and coping strategies that perpetuate harm. This creates a harmful loop of habits and mindsets stemming from the original trauma.

If a person does not break this unhealthy cycle by directly confronting their trauma, it can result in numerous harmful consequences. These may include the development of anxiety, depression, addiction, relationship difficulties, and more.

Therefore, it's essential to seek help and dedicate oneself to processing and overcoming emotional trauma. Without doing so, one risks becoming trapped in a harmful cycle, and the unchecked consequences can severely impact mental health, self-esteem, and overall well-being.

The main point is that unaddressed wounds continue to fuel this damaging cycle. Failure to escape this unhealthy pattern can lead to serious negative consequences in all aspects of life, as illustrated in the following story of King David.

King David's Astonishing Failure

King David, one of the most respected leaders in Israel's history, continues to be admired today. However, despite his strong connection to God, he was not without his significant errors. At times, David made choices that went against moral values.

One of David's most egregious mistakes occurred when he had an affair with Bathsheba, the wife of Uriah, one of his devoted soldiers. In a moment of weakness, David prioritized his desires over the sanctity of marriage. When Bathsheba became pregnant, he attempted to conceal his wrongdoing through deception.

David initially tried to bring Uriah back from the battlefield, hoping he would spend time with Bathsheba and assume the child was his. However, Uriah remained dedicated to his duty and refused to go home, choosing instead to sleep at the palace entrance near his fellow soldiers still engaged in combat.

When this plan failed, David resorted to more sinister measures. Unable to conceal his affair and Bathsheba's pregnancy, he ordered Uriah to be placed in the most dangerous part of the battle, effectively condemning him to death.

After Uriah was killed, David hastily married Bathsheba, believing he had successfully hidden his wrongdoing. However, the truth could not remain hidden. David's willingness to manipulate the battlefield and orchestrate Uriah's death to escape the consequences of his actions revealed the extent to which he would go to protect his own interests.

The Exposing of King David's Sins

In 2 Samuel 12, God sent the prophet Nathan to confront David about his sins. Nathan boldly addressed David's adultery with Bathsheba and his role in Uriah's death, making it clear God was fully aware of David's immoral actions and their corruption. Nathan warned David about the severe consequences he would face for damaging his reputation as a king.

When David realized his sins were exposed before God, he quickly confessed, "I have sinned greatly." His swift recognition of the situation demonstrated he understood the seriousness of his actions and marked the first step toward repentance, seeking forgiveness and renewal.

Accountability and Consequences

Nathan informed David that, while God had forgiven him, there would still be serious consequences. These consequences manifested in David's later years.

The Bible expresses David's profound remorse and sorrow in Psalm 51, which he wrote after these events. In this psalm, David pleaded, "Create in me a clean heart, O God, and renew a right and steadfast spirit within me."

David's use of the Hebrew verb bara, meaning "create," establishes a strong connection to God's act of creation. This word choice highlights David's longing for more than a superficial change. He sought a total transformation of his spiritual self, not just to erase his past mistakes, but to rebuild his moral understanding and character. This deeply emotional expression emphasizes the seriousness of David's repentance and his commitment to a journey of transformation toward redemption and renewal.

David's story powerfully reminds us that the damaging effects of unresolved emotional pain can affect anyone, even the "man after God's own heart." The question is: How could a man with such a profound love for God commit such a despicable act? The answer is simple yet complex: unhealed emotional trauma.

David's Sinful Actions: A Mirror of His Past

David's sin of taking Bathsheba as his wife strikingly echoed—though in a far more grievous way—the wrong done to him years earlier by King Saul. Saul had promised David his eldest daughter, Merab, as a reward for defeating Israel's enemies. Despite David fulfilling his part by achieving a decisive victory over the Philistines, Saul broke his promise and gave Merab to another man.

Driven by envy and fear of David's growing popularity, Saul viewed him as a threat to his throne. Later, Saul offered his younger daughter, Michal, to David but tied the marriage to a perilous condition: David had to bring back one hundred Philistine foreskins. Saul hoped this dangerous mission would lead to David's death. Yet, David succeeded, and Saul reluctantly gave Michal to him in marriage.

Even after this, Saul's jealousy persisted. He eventually took Michal away from David and gave her to another man—a betrayal that followed his repeated, failed attempts to kill David.

David endured the heartbreak of losing two promised wives, one of whom he had already married. This occurred when he was likely in his early twenties. By the time he became king at thirty, he had spent much of his youth fleeing Saul and fighting Israel's enemies.

When David finally ascended to the throne, Saul was dead, and David had secured the kingdom. God's blessing was evident in David's life—he was victorious in battle, prosperous, and had multiple wives and concubines.

However, despite these blessings, David committed an even greater betrayal. The man who had suffered the pain of losing his wives to others' schemes inflicted an unspeakable wound on one of his most loyal soldiers, Uriah. This raises a profound question: How could someone so familiar with betrayal and heartbreak choose to perpetuate such harm?

The answer lies in a simple yet powerful truth: hurting people, hurt others. Those with unhealed emotional wounds often, consciously or unconsciously, repeat the cycle of hurt. Though they may despise such acts, unresolved pain can lead even the most well-intentioned individuals to perpetuate the very harm they once endured.

Psychological studies support this notion. For instance, individuals who witness or experience abuse in childhood are statistically more likely to replicate such behaviors in their adult relationships. This understanding does not excuse David's immoral choices, but sheds light on how unresolved trauma can impair moral decision-making.

David's actions underscore the importance of breaking the cycle of pain by acknowledging past wounds, seeking healing, and cultivating healthier patterns. Processing emotional scars is crucial for preventing the perpetuation of harmful behaviors.

A Suppressed Conscience

Why didn't David's conscience trouble him about his sins until the prophet Nathan directly confronted him? One plausible explanation is cognitive dissonance—a psychological phenomenon where an individual experiences tension from holding contradictory beliefs or values.

David undoubtedly knew his actions toward Bathsheba and Uriah were immoral. Yet, as king, he may have engaged in mental gymnastics to rationalize his behavior, suppressing his conscience to avoid discomfort. His position of power could have fostered a sense of entitlement and invulnerability, further distorting his moral compass.

David's story reminds us that unchecked power and unprocessed pain can lead to devastating choices. However, his eventual repentance illustrates that transformation is possible.

David committed adultery with Bathsheba and arranged for the death of her husband, Uriah. However, David's heart was moved to repentance when the prophet Nathan confronted him. At that moment, David humbled himself, acknowledged his sin, and cried out to God for forgiveness and restoration. And God forgave him.

This is a perfect illustration of how the Lord rejoices in redeeming those who approach Him with a humble heart. Despite the serious consequences of David's actions, God's mercy was even greater. He forgave David and continued to use him powerfully, allowing him to write many of the cherished Psalms that have sustained the faith of God's people for generations.

Lessons to Draw From This Story

What lessons can we learn from this extraordinary story? How can we avoid repeating David's mistakes by allowing unresolved pain to derail our good intentions?

The first step is to bravely reflect on our emotions. Are there past wounds—perhaps from childhood, relationships, or ministry—that we have been ignoring or downplaying? Do we feel entitled to happiness and fulfillment, even if it means disregarding our obedience to God? These are challenging questions, but they are essential to confront if we want to live fully and honor the Lord.

Once we've identified our areas of emotional brokenness, we must bring them to Jesus' feet, trusting Him to do the deep inner work of healing and restoration.

This may involve seeking counsel from godly mentors, engaging in biblical counseling, or spending concentrated time in prayer and Scripture meditation. Regardless of the process, the key is allowing the Great Physician to tenderly address the root causes of our pain.

Yielding to the Holy Spirit

When we yield to the Holy Spirit's work, we will undergo a significant transformation. God's truth will replace the false beliefs we hold about ourselves and our situations.

In time, bitterness, resentment, and a sense of entitlement will be replaced by humility, grace, and a steadfast trust in our Heavenly Father's loving sovereignty.

When our hearts are aligned in this way, we will find the strength to make tough decisions that honor the Lord, even if they require significant personal sacrifice. We will be less vulnerable to the temptations that trapped David, as our identity, worth, and contentment will be securely established in Christ alone.

And like David, if we stumble, we'll be quick to repent and embrace the restoration God freely offers.

The Journey of Emotional Healing

My friend, the journey of emotional healing is not effortless, but it is essential for anyone desiring to walk closely with the Lord. This journey often requires us to muster the courage to confront our inner wounds, giving us the opportunity to understand the depth of our struggles and the resilience of our spirit. Like David, we may confront some dark and shameful aspects of our past, but it is through this confrontation that we can begin to discern the lessons and growth hidden within those experiences.

However, as we bring those wounds into the light of God's love, we'll experience the miraculous transformation that comes solely from the redeeming power of the cross. In this process, we can find hope and renewal, knowing that each step taken towards healing is a step closer to embracing the fullness of life that God offers. Ultimately, this journey not only enriches our relationship with the Lord but also empowers us to extend compassion and understanding to others who may

David's narrative serves as a compelling illustration of God's grace and the transformative power of repentance. His journey exemplifies how acknowledging our shortcomings and turning back to God can lead to profound changes within us. When we yield to the Holy Spirit's work, we will undergo a significant transformation that reshapes not only our mindset but also our entire life direction. God's truth will replace the false beliefs we hold about ourselves and our situations, allowing us to see ourselves through His eyes.

Over time, bitterness, resentment, and a sense of entitlement will be replaced by humility, grace, and a steadfast trust in our Heavenly Father's loving sovereignty. This process of renewal is not instantaneous; rather, it unfolds gradually, revealing the depths of God's mercy and compassion as we walk in faith. As we embrace this journey, we become more aware of the divine purpose for our lives, which ultimately fosters deeper connections with others and enriches our spiritual growth.

The Power of Repentance

Although David made significant mistakes, his readiness to admit them, repent, and pursue moral renewal highlights the transformative impact of remorse. His actions illustrate that true repentance and a dedication to personal growth can result in positive change.

God has blessed us with the gift and opportunity of repentance. When we truly grasp the effectiveness of genuine repentance and the risks associated with failing to repent, we will seek it with the respect it deserves.

In the upcoming chapter, we will explore the role of repentance in the process of transformation.

CHAPTER 19

OVERCOMING "NEGATIVE 'SELF-TALK'

As stated previously, that inner critic - the voice in your mind - can often be harsh and unforgiving. While our Christian faith calls us to share God's love and hope with those around us, we sometimes forget a crucial truth: we also need to extend that same love and grace to ourselves.

This journey of breaking free from negative self-talk is about aligning your thoughts with God's truth, recognizing His voice within, and living in the fullness of who He created you to be.

Negative Self-Talk: The Battle Within

Think about your day yesterday. Did you catch yourself thinking or saying things like:

"I can't do this."

"I'm not good enough."

"Why do I even bother?"

Many of us engage in this kind of self-talk without even realizing it. Often, we are harder on ourselves than we would ever dream of being on a loved one. But is this how God wants us to treat ourselves—the masterpiece He created in His own image?

In Matthew 12:36-37, Jesus reminds us of the power of words:

"But I tell you that everyone will have to give an account on the day of judgment for every empty word they have spoken. For by your words you will be acquitted, and by your words you will be condemned."

This truth doesn't just apply to the words we speak to others, but also to the words we speak to ourselves. Negative self-talk isn't just a harmless habit; it's agreeing with lies that contradict God's Word about who we are.

Examining Negative Self-Talk

Negative self-talk is like having an internal critic that magnifies your flaws and minimizes your strengths. Here are some common examples:

"I'll never be good enough."

"Everyone else is better than me."

"I always mess things up."

"God probably doesn't even care about me."

These thoughts feel powerful and convincing in the moment, but they're rooted in lies. God's Word offers a vastly different narrative about your identity and worth.

Common Sources of Negative Self-Talk

Past Experience: Words spoken over us in childhood or past failures can leave deep wounds that resurface as self-criticism.

Cultural Pressures: Society often sets unattainable standards for success, beauty, or intelligence, leaving us feeling inadequate.

Spiritual Warfare: The enemy thrives on planting seeds of doubt, fear, and insecurity, hoping you'll forget God's truth.

The Destructive Impact of Negative Self-Talk

Negative self-talk doesn't just exist in your mind; it influences every aspect of your life:

Mental Health:

Constant self-criticism is like a slow-dripping poison to your mind. It fuels anxiety, depression, and feelings of unworthiness. But Jesus offers peace and joy:

"Peace I leave with you; my peace I give you. I do not give to you as the world gives. Do not let your hearts be troubled and do not be afraid" (John 14:27).

Relationships: Negative self-talk can lead to destructive patterns: You might push others away, believing you're unworthy of love or connection. Alternatively, you might settle for unhealthy relationships, thinking you don't deserve better.

When we see ourselves through God's eyes, we can approach relationships with confidence and grace.

Dreams and Goals: Have you ever let a dream die because of fear or self-doubt? Perhaps you wanted to start a new career, pursue a ministry, or develop a talent, but that inner voice said, "You'll fail."

"For I know the plans I have for you," declares the Lord, "plans to prosper you and not to harm you, plans to give you hope and a future" (Jeremiah 29:11).

Truth vs. Negative Self-Talk

When we believe lies about ourselves, we disagree with God's Word. Let's contrast common negative self-talk with God's truth:

Negative Self-Talk: "I'm worthless." Truth: "You are fearfully and wonderfully made" (Psalm 139:14).

Negative Self-Talk: "I can't do this." Truth: "I can do all things through Christ who strengthens me" (Philippians 4:13).

Negative Self-Talk: "Nobody loves me." Truth: "I have loved you with an everlasting love" (Jeremiah 31:3).

Negative Self-Talk: "I always fail." Truth: "In all these things, we are more than conquerors through him who loved us" (Romans 8:37).

Breaking Free: Actionable Steps

Catch Your Thoughts:

Start paying attention to what you say to yourself. Ask:

Would I say this to a close friend?

Does this thought align with God's Word?

Replace lies with truths from Scripture.

Replace Lies with Truth: Memorize verses and create affirmations, such as:

"I am loved unconditionally by God."

"I am chosen and called for a purpose."

Practice Gratitude: Write down three things you're thankful for daily.

Pray for Renewal: Ask God to renew your mind and replace critical thoughts with His affirming truth.

Surround Yourself with Encouragement:

Lean on trusted friends, mentors, or counselors.

Staying Free: Building New Habits

Regular Thought Checks: "Above all else, guard your heart, for everything you do flows from it" (Proverbs 4:23).

Speak Life: "The tongue has the power of life and death" (Proverbs 18:21).

Celebrate Progress: Every step forward is a victory.

A Challenge for the Week

Thought Journal: Write down negative thoughts and replace them with Scripture.

Daily Affirmations:

Speak positive truths each morning.

Share with a Friend: Discuss your progress for encouragement.

Seeing Yourself Through God's Eyes

Breaking free from negative self-talk isn't just about improving your mood—it's about embracing the abundant life Jesus died to give you. When you see yourself through God's eyes, you'll realize that you are His masterpiece, equipped and empowered to live out His purpose for your life.

In the next chapter, we explore the story of a man named Jabez, who learned to overcome the negative name given to him at birth. This name contributed to a poor self-image and significantly damaged his identity as a servant of God. Only when he began to see his identity and value through God's eyes was he able to break free from his negative self-image.

CHAPTER 20

THE STORY OF JABEZ

The story of Jabez is one of transformation, faith, and the power of divine realization. Found in 1 Chronicles 4:9-10, his brief narrative shines a profound light on how a person can rise above unfavorable circumstances and self-imposed limitations through faith and reliance on God. Jabez's journey from internal conflict to spiritual breakthrough serves as an inspiration for all believers, reminding us of our own identity as heirs to God's promises and the blessings of the covenant.

The Weight of A Name

The passage begins by telling us that Jabez was "more honorable than his brothers." This description highlights his strong moral principles, ethical behavior, and commitment to living a life that benefited others. However, despite being regarded as honorable by those around him, Jabez carried a deep and personal struggle rooted in his very name. His mother named him "Jabez," meaning "one who causes pain," because of the hardship she endured during his birth. In the ancient world, names carried significant meaning, often shaping a person's identity and destiny.

Imagine growing up with a name that constantly reminded you—and everyone else—of sorrow and pain. It's not hard to see how this could foster a negative self-image. For Jabez, this name became a label that harmed his self-esteem, limited his personal achievements, and deprived him of joy and peace. Though others admired Jabez for his honor and integrity, he struggled to appreciate himself. Shame, feelings of inadequacy, and a sense of being cursed marred his self-perception.

This internal battle was a heavy burden. Jabez likely questioned his worth and wondered if he was destined to live a life filled with pain and limitation. Such feelings, if left unaddressed, can derail even the most honorable of lives.

The Turning Point

For Jabez, the turning point came when the pain and frustration became unbearable. It was this sense of desperation that gave birth to conviction. He began to see that his current state was not aligned with God's will for his life. The realization that he was meant for more ignited a boldness in Jabez, driving him to seek change.

Jabez came to understand that as a descendant of Abraham; he was entitled to the blessings of the covenant—a divine promise of prosperity, protection, and purpose.

Jabez cried out to the God of Israel, praying with boldness and specificity.

"Oh, that you would bless me and enlarge my territory! Let your hand be with me and keep me from harm so that I will be free from pain" (1 Chronicles 4:10, NIV).

This prayer is remarkable because it encapsulates the essence of faith. Jabez didn't approach God with timid or vague requests. He prayed with the assurance that God was both willing and able to bless him. This wasn't a prayer of selfish ambition, but one rooted in a deep trust in God's goodness.

Why Enlarge the Territory?

Jabez's request to enlarge his territory was a visionary act of faith. In his time, land represented more than just physical space—it was a symbol of prosperity, influence, and the capacity to steward God's blessings. Despite his current limitations, Jabez believed God had greater things in store for him. He saw an expanded territory not only as a tangible resource but also as an opportunity to live in alignment with the covenant blessings promised to Abraham and his descendants.

This request was more than practical; it was deeply spiritual. By asking God to enlarge his territory, Jabez was declaring his trust in God's provision and his readiness to embrace a greater role in fulfilling God's purpose. He anticipated abundant blessings and prepared himself to receive them, demonstrating a mindset of faith and expectancy.

The Abrahamic Connection and Believers Today

Jabez's prayer and transformation are rooted in the Abrahamic Covenant, which is foundational to the faith journey of God's people. In Genesis 12:1-3, God promised Abraham:

"I will make you into a great nation, and I will bless you; I will make your name great, and you will be a blessing... and all peoples on earth will be blessed through you." (NIV)

This covenant established a legacy of blessings for Abraham and his descendants, encompassing prosperity, protection, and divine favor. Jabez's realization of his identity as a descendant of Abraham was the key to his transformation. He recognized he was not destined to live a life defined by pain and limitation, but was entitled to the blessings of the covenant.

Today, believers are also heirs to the promises of the Abrahamic Covenant. Through faith in Jesus Christ, we are grafted into this covenant and become spiritual descendants of Abraham. As Galatians 3:29 declares:

"If you belong to Christ, then you are Abraham's seed, and heirs according to the promise" (NIV).

This truth is transformative. Just as Jabez claimed his identity and sought God's blessings, we, too, can approach God with boldness, knowing that we are entitled to the blessings of the covenant. The promises of prosperity, protection, and purpose are available to all who believe and walk in faith.

The Internal Conflict of Jabez

Jabez's struggle with his self-perception offers valuable insights into the nature of internal conflict. Though he was regarded as honorable by others, Jabez's internal dialogue likely told a different story. He may have felt unworthy of blessings, burdened by his name and the circumstances of his birth.

This kind of conflict is not unique to Jabez. Many people, even those who appear outwardly successful, wrestle with feelings of inadequacy, shame, and unworthiness. These inner battles can create barriers to receiving God's blessings, as they cause us to doubt His goodness and our place in His plan.

Jabez's breakthrough came when he chose to confront his internal conflict head-on. Instead of allowing his negative self-perception to define him, he brought his pain and limitations to God. His prayer was an act of surrender, a declaration that he would no longer be bound by his past or his name.

Jabez: From Pain to Purpose

The Bible concludes Jabez's story with a simple yet powerful statement: "And God granted his request" (1 Chronicles 4:10, NIV). This response speaks volumes about the nature of God. He is a loving Father who delights in blessing His children and answering prayers that align with His will.

For Jabez, this resolution was immediate and transformative. His prayer for blessings, an enlarged territory, and protection from harm was granted, marking a dramatic shift in his life. What had once been a source of pain and limitation became a testimony to God's goodness and faithfulness.

Parallels with Other Biblical Characters

Jabez's story is echoed in the lives of other biblical characters who experienced transformation through faith and the realization of their identity in God.

Jacob: From Deceiver to Israel

Jacob, whose name means "supplanter" or "deceiver," wrestled with God and received a new name: Israel, meaning "he struggles with God" (Genesis 32:28). Like Jabez, Jacob had to confront his identity and embrace God's purpose for his life.

The Woman with the Issue of Blood

In Mark 5, a woman suffering from a debilitating condition for twelve years reached out in faith to touch Jesus' garment. Jesus declared, "Daugh-

ter (of Abraham, entitled to the Blessing), your faith has healed you."
This declaration restored her identity and dignity, much like Jabez's prayer
restored his sense of worth.

Gideon: From Fear to Courage

Gideon, in Judges 6, saw himself as the least of his family. But when
the angel of the Lord called him a "mighty warrior," Gideon's perspective
changed. Like Jabez, Gideon had to overcome a negative self-image and
step into his God-given purpose.

Application for Believers Today

Jabez's story transcends time, offering practical and spiritual lessons for
every believer seeking transformation. His journey reminds us that change
begins with an inner shift—recognizing who we are in Christ and boldly
approaching God with faith and expectancy. Here are four key takeaways
for applying Jabez's story to our lives:

1. Claim Your Identity in Christ

Like Jabez, we are heirs to God's promises. Through faith in Jesus
Christ, we are grafted into the Abrahamic Covenant and entitled to its
blessings. The Apostle Paul emphasizes this in Galatians 3:29:

"If you belong to Christ, then you are Abraham's seed, and heirs according to the promise." (NIV)

This truth is foundational to our faith. It reminds us that we are not
defined by our past, our circumstances, or the labels others have placed on
us. Instead, our identity is rooted in God's promises—promises of favor,
protection, prosperity, and purpose. Embracing this identity empowers us

to approach God with boldness and live with confidence in His plans for us.

Jabez's transformation began with the realization that he was not destined for a life of pain and limitation. Similarly, when we recognize our spiritual heritage and claim our identity in Christ, we open the door for God to work powerfully in our lives.

2. Pray Boldly and Specifically

One of the most striking aspects of Jabez's story is the boldness and specificity of his prayer. He didn't approach God with vague or timid requests. Instead, he asked for blessing, expansion, guidance, and protection—trusting that God would grant his desires.

"Oh, that you would bless me and enlarge my territory! Let your hand be with me and keep me from harm so that I will be free from pain." (1 Chronicles 4:10 (NIV)

This prayer reflects Jabez's deep faith in God's ability to transform his circumstances. It also demonstrates the importance of praying with clarity and purpose. When we bring our needs and desires to God, we should do so with confidence, knowing that He hears us and delights in answering prayers that align with His will.

Jesus encouraged this kind of bold prayer in Matthew 7:7:

"Ask and it will be given to you; seek and you will find; knock and the door will be opened to you." (NIV)

Praying boldly is an act of faith. It acknowledges God's sovereignty and invites Him to move in ways that exceed our expectations. Like Jabez, we should approach God with specific requests, trusting that He will provide exactly what we need.

3. Address Internal Conflict

Jabez's story highlights the importance of addressing the internal conflicts that can hinder our growth and transformation. Despite being described as "more honorable than his brothers," Jabez struggled with a negative self-perception rooted in his name and the circumstances of his birth. This internal battle limited his ability to fully embrace his potential and live with joy and peace.

Transformation requires more than external change; it involves inner healing. As Proverbs 4:23 reminds us:

"Above all else, guard your heart, for everything you do flows from it." (NIV)

To experience true transformation, we must be intentional about addressing unresolved pain, negative thoughts, and limiting beliefs. This process often involves bringing our struggles to God in prayer, seeking His healing and restoration. Psalm 34:18 offers reassurance for this journey:

"The Lord is close to the brokenhearted and saves those who are crushed in spirit." (NIV)

Like Jabez, we can overcome internal conflict by surrendering our pain and limitations to God. His love and grace have the power to heal our wounds, renew our minds, and restore our sense of worth.

4. Expect God's Goodness

Jabez's faith was rooted in the belief that God desired to bless him. This expectation of God's goodness was the driving force behind his bold prayer and his trust in God's ability to answer it. As believers, we are called to have the same confident expectation of God's goodness.

The Bible is filled with promises that affirm God's desire to bless His children. In Jeremiah 29:11, God declares:

"For I know the plans I have for you," declares the Lord, "plans to prosper you and not to harm you, plans to give you hope and a future." (NIV)

This verse reminds us that God's plans for us are always for our good. When we pray and step out in faith, we can trust that He will provide, protect, and guide us according to His perfect will.

Expecting God's goodness also means living with gratitude and a heart of worship. As we receive His blessings, we are called to share them with others, becoming conduits of His grace and love.

Conclusion

The story of Jabez is a testament to the power of faith, prayer, and divine transformation. It reminds us that no matter how painful or limiting our past may be; we serve a God who specializes in rewriting stories. Jabez's name, which once symbolized pain, became a testimony to God's ability to bring healing and restoration.

As believers, we are invited to step into our covenant identity, claim the promises of God, and approach Him with bold and specific prayers. Like Jabez, we can trust that God is faithful to answer our cries, enlarge our vision, and guide us into a future filled with purpose and blessing.

Prayer for Transformation and Blessing

Heavenly Father,

Thank You for Your unfailing love, faithfulness, and the promises You have given to Your children. Like Jabez, I come to You with boldness and humility, seeking Your divine touch in every area of my life.

Lord, I ask that You bless me abundantly—not just with material things, but with spiritual growth, wisdom, peace, and joy. Enlarge my territory, Father, expanding my influence, opportunities, and capacity to serve others for Your glory. Help me to steward well the blessings You pour into my life and use them to bring honor to Your name.

Let Your hand be with me, guiding my steps and protecting me from harm. Keep me from the pain of past wounds and negative self-perceptions that try to hold me back. Heal the areas of my heart that are broken, and renew my mind so I can see myself as You see me—beloved, chosen, and equipped for Your purpose.

Lord, help me to claim my identity in Christ and walk in the promises of the covenant You made with Abraham, knowing that through Jesus, I am a spiritual heir to every blessing. Fill me with faith to trust Your goodness and courage to pursue the vision You have for my life.

I surrender all to You, Lord, believing that You will transform my circumstances, heal my heart, and lead me into a future of hope, abundance, and purpose. Thank You for hearing my prayer and for being a God who answers.

In Jesus' name, I pray. Amen.

Repentance: The Foundation Of Transformation

Jabez's story is a powerful testament to the transformative power of faith and divine intervention. However, his journey did not begin with an immediate breakthrough; it started with a profound internal shift. Jabez had to confront and repent of his lack of faith in God's promises, a repentance deeply rooted in the negative connotations of his name. By acknowledging his limitations and surrendering his preconceived notions, Jabez opened the door for God's blessings to flow into his life. This act of repentance was not merely a momentary confession but a heartfelt turning away from doubt and self-imposed barriers towards unwavering trust in God's covenant.

Repentance played a crucial role in Jabez's transformation. It was the catalyst that allowed his heart to be changed and his mind to be renewed. Without this essential step, the profound change he experienced would not have been possible. Just as Jabez had to let go of his internal struggles and repent of his fears, we too must embrace repentance as a foundational element in our own journeys toward transformation. Repentance clears the path for God to work in our lives, enabling us to shed old, limiting patterns and embrace the abundant life He has promised.

In the upcoming chapter, we will discuss the powerful and necessary role of repentance in the transformation journey.

CHAPTER 21

THE ROLE OF REPENTANCE IN PERSONAL GROWTH

Repentance: The Foundation of Transformation

Repentance plays a powerful and life-changing role in personal and spiritual transformation, and it was undoubtedly a pivotal aspect of Jabez's journey.

Repentance is not merely about confessing wrongdoings; it involves a deep and genuine change of heart and mind—a reorientation of one's thoughts, beliefs, and actions toward God's truth and purpose. Jabez's transformation was marked by his ability to acknowledge his internal struggles, turn to God in humility, and align his desires with God's will.

True repentance isn't just about changing your actions. It requires a genuine change of heart and mind—a new way of thinking and a sincere desire to improve.

This kind of transformation is deep and shapes who you are at your core. It involves letting go of past mistakes and harmful patterns that have been holding you back, leading to forgiveness, closure, and a fresh start.

The Transformative Power of Repentance

God, in His infinite love and mercy, has extended to us the incredible gift of repentance—a divine opportunity to realign ourselves with His perfect will. Repentance is not a punishment or a task to dread, but a pathway to restoration and renewal. It offers freedom from guilt, healing for our wounded souls, and reconciliation in our relationship with God.

When we grasp the depth of this gift, we see repentance not as a chore but as a privilege and an act of worship. It is our response to God's boundless grace and mercy, a way to draw nearer to His heart.

Repentance is more than uttering words of apology or regret; it is a transformative experience that touches the deepest parts of who we are. It requires more than just turning away from sin—it is about turning toward God.

Genuine repentance involves a change in both mind and heart, a sincere commitment to leave behind the behaviors, attitudes, and patterns that separate us from Him. It's about inviting God into the broken places of our lives and allowing Him to reshape, restore, and renew us.

Repentance and God's Forgiveness

One of the most beautiful truths about repentance is that it leads us to experience the fullness of God's forgiveness. In 1 John 1:9, the Bible reminds us, "If we confess our sins, He is faithful and just to forgive us our sins and to cleanse us from all unrighteousness" (NKJV).

This promise assures us that when we come to God in humility, acknowledging our sins and asking for His forgiveness, He not only pardons us but also cleanses us completely.

God's forgiveness is not partial or conditional. It is total, and it is imme-diate. He does not hold our past sins against us like a shadow of condem-nation. Instead, He removes them as far as the east is from the west (Psalm 103:12). Repentance allows us to step into this reality, freeing us from the chains of guilt and shame that often keep us bound.

Yet, many of us hesitate to repent because we fear rejection. We wonder, "Will God really forgive me after what I've done?" But Scripture repeatedly affirms that no sin is too great for God's mercy. David, after committing adultery with Bathsheba and orchestrating the death of her husband, cried out in Psalm 51:1-2, "Have mercy on me, O God, according to Your lovingkindness; according to the multitude of Your tender mercies, blot out my transgressions. Wash me thoroughly from my iniquity, and cleanse me from my sin" (NKJV).

David's repentance was met with God's forgiveness, showing us that His grace can cover even our gravest sins when we approach Him with a contrite heart.

The Heart of Repentance

True repentance begins in the heart. It is not simply a matter of chang-ing external behaviors, but of experiencing an inward transformation. As Ezekiel 36:26 promises, "I will give you a new heart and put a new spirit within you; I will take the heart of stone out of your flesh and give you a heart of flesh" (NKJV).

Repentance softens our hearts, making them receptive to God's love and guidance.

This inward change involves recognizing the seriousness of sin and un-derstanding how it grieves the heart of God. Repentance is not merely about feeling sorry for the consequences of our actions; it is about sorrow for the sin itself. The Apostle Paul describes this as "godly sorrow," which leads to repentance and brings about salvation without regret (2 Corinthians 7:10). Godly sorrow compels us to turn away from sin, not out of fear of punishment, but out of love and reverence for God.

This kind of repentance requires humility. It means admitting that we have fallen short, that we are incapable of saving ourselves, and that we need God's help to change. It is in this place of humility that God meets us with His grace. As James 4:6 reminds us, "God resists the proud, but gives grace to the humble" (NKJV).

The Risks of Un-Repentance

While repentance is a gift, neglecting it carries significant risks. Unrepented sin creates a barrier between us and God, hindering our spiritual growth and dulling our sensitivity to His voice. Isaiah 59:2 warns, "Your iniquities have separated you from your God; and your sins have hidden His face from you, so that He will not hear" (NKJV).

This separation is not because God moves away from us, but because sin hardens our hearts and prevents us from experiencing the fullness of His presence.

Over time, ignoring the call to repent can lead to spiritual stagnation. Our conscience becomes desensitized, and we risk becoming comfortable with sin. This state is dangerous because it blinds us to the need for change. Proverbs 28:13 says, "He who covers his sins will not prosper, but whoever confesses and forsakes them will have mercy" (NKJV).

Without repentance, we remain stuck in cycles of guilt, shame, and disobedience, unable to experience the freedom and joy that comes from walking in God's grace.

Repentance and Transformation

Repentance is not only about forgiveness, but also about transformation. When we repent, we open ourselves to God's work in our lives, allowing Him to mold us into the people He created us to be. Romans 12:2 urges us, "Do not be conformed to this world, but be transformed by the renewing of your mind" (NKJV). Repentance initiates this renewal, enabling us to break free from old patterns and step into the new life God has prepared for us.

Through repentance, we learn to see sin as God sees it. We desire what He desires and to align our will with His. This alignment leads to lasting change, not because we strive in our own strength, but because we rely on His power working within us. Philippians 2:13 reminds us, "It is God who works in you both to will and to do for His good pleasure" (NKJV). Repentance invites God into our struggles, empowering us to overcome sin and live victoriously.

A Daily Practice

Repentance is not a one-time event; it is an ongoing practice. As believers, we are called to examine our hearts regularly and turn to God whenever we fall short. Lamentations 3:22-23 reminds us that God's mercies are new every morning, giving us the opportunity to start fresh each day. This daily act of repentance keeps our hearts tender and our relationship with God strong.

Repentance also teaches us humility and dependence. It reminds us that we are not perfect and that we need God's grace every step of the way. As Proverbs 3:5-6 encourages, "Trust in the Lord with all your heart, and lean not on your own understanding; in all your ways acknowledge Him, and

He shall direct your paths" (NKJV). When we practice repentance daily, we invite God to guide and shape our lives according to His will.

The Fruit of Repentance

The fruit of repentance is evident in a transformed life. When we turn from sin and align ourselves with God, we experience peace, joy, and spiritual growth. We become more compassionate, more forgiving, and more like Christ. Our relationships improve as we learn to admit our mistakes and seek reconciliation. Our witness to others becomes stronger as they see the power of God's grace at work in us.

John the Baptist called for "fruits worthy of repentance" (Luke 3:8, NKJV), reminding us that true repentance produces visible change. It is not enough to say we have repented; our actions must reflect the sincerity of our hearts. This fruit is a testament to the transformative power of God's grace and a witness to the world of His love and mercy.

The Throne of Grace: A Safe Haven for Believers in Times of Failure

Hebrews 4:16 reminds us: "Let us therefore come boldly to the throne of grace, that we may obtain mercy and find grace to help in time of need" (NKJV). This verse offers hope to believers who fail in their walk with God. It speaks directly to those weighed down by guilt and shame, reassuring them that God's throne of grace is always open, even in their moments of failure.

The "throne of grace" is not reserved for the perfect or the sinless. It is for those who stumble and fall, those who struggle to live out their faith.

It is where we find God's mercy and strength to rise again, no matter how many times we fail.

Grace: God's Mercy for Our Shortcomings

When believers fail, it's easy to feel unworthy of God's presence. We may hesitate to come to Him, fearing judgment or rejection. Yet the throne of grace is a place of mercy. Mercy means that God doesn't give us the punishment we deserve; instead, He offers forgiveness, compassion, and a chance to start over.

The Bible gives us many examples of God extending mercy to those who failed. Consider Peter, who denied Jesus three times in His hour of greatest need. Despite Peter's failure, Jesus didn't reject him. Instead, He forgave and restored Peter, entrusting him with the mission of leading His church. Like Peter, we can approach God with our failures, knowing He is ready to forgive and restore us when we come with a repentant heart.

As Psalm 103:10-12 says, "He does not treat us as our sins deserve or repay us according to our iniquities. For as high as the heavens are above the earth, so great is His love for those who fear Him; as far as the east is from the west, so far has He removed our transgressions from us," (NIV). God's mercy is limitless, and it is always available to those who seek Him.

Grace to Rise Again

While mercy forgives our failures, grace empowers us to move forward. Many times, failure leaves us feeling defeated and unworthy. But the throne of grace reminds us that God's strength is made perfect in our weakness (2 Corinthians 12:9). Grace gives us the power to stand up after we fall and to continue walking in faith, even when it feels hard.

God's grace is not just unearned favor, but also the divine strength that empowers us to conquer our weaknesses. When we come to God after failing, He meets us with grace, equipping us to face life's challenges with renewed confidence in His power.

Come Boldly

Hebrews 4:16 encourages us to approach the throne of grace boldly. This boldness is not arrogance or entitlement; it is the confidence that comes from knowing we are His children. Our boldness is rooted in the finished work of Jesus Christ, who paid the price for our sins and secured our access to the Father.

Through Jesus, we are not outsiders but sons and daughters of God. Ephesians 3:12 says, "In Him and through faith in Him we may approach God with freedom and confidence" (NIV). Even in failure, we can approach God, knowing He welcomes us with open arms.

The Risk of Avoiding the Throne

Failing to come to the throne of grace can have significant consequences. When we avoid God because of guilt or shame, we miss out on the mercy and grace that He freely offers. Instead, we may find ourselves stuck in cycles of regret, fear, and spiritual stagnation.

Unrepented failure can harden our hearts and distance us from God, but He never moves away from us. He patiently waits for us to return to Him. Isaiah 1:18 reminds us of God's invitation: "Come now, let us reason together," says the Lord. "Though your sins are like scarlet, they shall be as white as snow; though they are red as crimson, they shall be like wool" (NIV).

Avoiding God after failure only prolongs the pain and prevents healing. Coming to the throne of grace, however, brings freedom, restoration, and peace.

The Place of Grace for the Struggling Believer

If you have failed in your walk with God, know this: the throne of grace is for you. It is not a place of condemnation, but a place of mercy and renewal. God does not turn His back on His children when they fail. Instead, He invites us to come to Him, lay down our burdens, and receive His forgiveness and strength.

The throne of grace reminds us that failure is not the end. Proverbs 24:16 says, "For though the righteous fall seven times, they rise again" (NIV). Your failures do not define you. God's mercy and grace are greater than your mistakes, and His power is sufficient to help you rise and continue walking in His purpose for your life.

Remember, God's throne is not a throne of judgment for believers, but a throne of grace. It is where we can bring our failures without fear and find the love, mercy, and strength we need to move forward. So come boldly—not because you are perfect, but because His grace is.

Repentance Is A Gift

Repentance is a gift that God has given us to bring us closer to Him, restore our relationships, and transform our lives. It is an opportunity to experience His forgiveness, healing, and grace significantly. While the risks of unrepentance are great, the rewards of genuine repentance are far greater. Through repentance, we find freedom, renewal, and the strength to live the life God has called us to live.

Let us not take this gift for granted. Instead, let us approach repentance with the respect and gratitude it deserves, allowing it to shape us into the people God created us to be. In the next chapter, we will explore how repentance plays a crucial role in the process of transformation, leading us to a deeper understanding of God's love and purpose for our lives.

Self-Awareness and Repentance

Understanding the importance of repentance and the continuous availability of the throne of grace should prompt us to reflect not only on our actions, but also on the deeper motivations that drive them.

As we come to God with our failures, seeking His mercy and grace, it is also an opportunity to pause and examine the root causes of our struggles. This act of introspection—paired with repentance—opens the door to greater self-awareness, which is a vital part of spiritual growth.

Self-awareness helps us move beyond simply addressing our failures and allows us to understand why we fail. It brings clarity to the patterns, habits, and inner thoughts that may lead us away from God's will. When we combine the gift of repentance with the practice of self-awareness, we position ourselves for true transformation—a lasting change that begins in the heart and flows into every area of our lives.

With this in mind, let us now explore the transformative impact of Self-Awareness, a powerful tool that works hand in hand with repentance to reshape our character and align us more closely with God's purpose.

CHAPTER 22

THE TRANSFORMATIVE IMPACT OF SELF-AWARENESS

Have you ever met someone who seemed completely unaware of how their actions affected others? Perhaps you've had a moment when you suddenly recognized something about yourself that you had never noticed before. These experiences highlight the significance and transformative power of self-awareness.

Self-awareness is like turning on a light in a dark room. Suddenly, you can see what was always there but hidden. As you grow more self-aware, you gain deeper insight into your thoughts, feelings, and behaviors. This understanding empowers you to make intentional changes in your life, aligning your choices with God's truth and purpose.

What Is Self-Awareness?

Self-awareness is the ability to recognize and understand consciously your own thoughts, emotions, and behaviors, as well as their impact on yourself and others. To put another way, self-awareness means understanding your own thoughts, emotions, and actions, and how they affect you and the surrounding people. When guided by the Holy Spirit, self-awareness helps you live according to God's plan, reflecting His image in your daily life.

Internal Self-Awareness Internal self-awareness is about knowing what's going on inside you—your feelings, motivations, and habits. The Holy Spirit can show you areas in your heart that need change, helping you grow closer to God's will for your life.

External Self-Awareness External self-awareness is about seeing yourself the way others see you. It helps you understand how your actions affect others and encourages you to respond with humility and kindness. With God's guidance, you can learn to treat others with the same love and care that Christ shows you.

Why Self-Awareness Matters?

Self-awareness is the foundation of personal and spiritual growth. When you can recognize where you need to improve, you can take steps to make changes. It helps you build stronger relationships, make better choices, and live a life led by faith instead of impulse. From a spiritual perspective, self-awareness allows you to see the truth about yourself—the good and the areas that need work. It prepares your heart to respond to the Holy Spirit, helping you align your life with God's plan.

A Biblical Perspective on Self-Awareness

The Bible encourages self-awareness as an essential part of a believer's journey with God. In Psalm 139:23–24 (NKJV), David prays: *"Search me, O God, and know my heart; try me, and know my anxieties; and see if there is any wicked way in me, and lead me in the way everlasting."*

Here, David shows that true self-awareness begins with God. It is through the Holy Spirit's guidance that we see our shortcomings—not to feel shame, but to grow. The Holy Spirit lovingly leads us toward repentance, righteousness, and grace.

Self-awareness in this context isn't about focusing on ourselves, but about becoming the person God created us to be. When we allow the Spirit to reveal the truth about our hearts, we take a step closer to living in alignment with God's purpose for our lives.

Self-Awareness and Repentance: The Role of the Holy Spirit

True repentance begins with honest self-awareness. Without recognizing sin, full repentance is impossible. The Holy Spirit's conviction is a loving gift that awakens us to harmful patterns and draws us closer to God. Instead of condemning, the Spirit gently prompts us to face the truth about our behavior. When met with humility, this conviction transforms hollow apologies into sincere confessions, paving the way for reconciliation with God and others.

The Power of Genuine Repentance

Genuine repentance requires a humble heart that fully acknowledges wrongdoing. David's prayer in Psalm 51 exemplifies this:

"Lord, I see my wrongdoing for what it is, and I turn away from it."

He takes full responsibility without blaming others or making excuses. This transparency invites God's grace, restores the relationship, and leads the believer toward renewal.

The Danger of Self-Deception

Without self-awareness, we risk walking blindly in self-deception. We may offer insincere apologies or ignore our faults, leaving no room for God's healing work. Proverbs 28:13 (NKJV) warns:

"He who covers his sins will not prosper, but whoever confesses and forsakes them will have mercy."

Choosing honest self-reflection over denial opens the door to divine mercy and genuine transformation.

Aligning Self-Awareness with Repentance

Invite the Holy Spirit to Search Your Heart: Humbly ask the Holy Spirit to reveal hidden sins or harmful patterns, following David's example.

Acknowledge Your Sin Without Excuses: Fully own your actions, avoiding vague or defensive language.

Turn Away from Sin and Toward God: With God's help, leave behind sinful habits and pursue righteousness.

Trust in God's Mercy and Grace: God is faithful to forgive and cleanse when you confess and forsake sin (1 John 1:9).

The Benefits of Self-Awareness and Repentance

When self-awareness leads to genuine repentance, it brings restored intimacy with God, freedom from guilt, and renewed joy.

The Holy Spirit reshapes your heart and mind to better reflect Christ. This transformation leads to a life filled with divine purpose, love, peace, and the fullness of God's grace.

Embracing the Journey of Self-Discovery

Becoming truly self-aware changes how you see yourself and the world. You begin to recognize blind spots and harmful patterns and find the insight needed for lasting change. By submitting your thoughts, emotions, and actions to God, you'll gain strength and wisdom to navigate life's challenges.

Growing in Self-Awareness Through Prayer

Deep self-awareness starts with prayerful reflection. In moments of stillness, invite the Holy Spirit to search your heart. He will reveal areas needing change and healing. Though this honesty can be difficult, it is also liberating. Facing these truths brings freedom and moves you closer to who God created you to be.

Embracing Vulnerability and Accountability in Community

Surround yourself with trustworthy, God-centered friends who can lovingly challenge and encourage you. These companions can help you see blind spots, confront destructive habits, and support you in breaking free from old patterns. In a Christ-centered community, you'll find the strength to grow, stepping boldly into God's plan for your life.

Living a Self-Aware Life: Guided by the Holy Spirit

Living self-aware means continually inviting the Holy Spirit to transform every part of your life. By renewing your mind through Scripture, prayer, and fellowship, you can overcome the lies of the enemy, recognize sin, and find healing for past wounds.

As your self-awareness deepens, your relationships will grow stronger, and your compassion for others will increase. A humble, teachable spirit keeps you on the path of growth and draws you closer to God's heart.

Looking Ahead

In the next chapter, we'll explore personal development and how self-awareness lays the foundation for growth and a deeper connection with our Heavenly Father.

CHAPTER 23

PERSONAL DEVELOPMENT: A JOURNEY OF FAITH AND GROWTH

Personal development is a lifelong journey of becoming the person God purpose you to be. It's not just about improving skills or achieving goals—it's about growing closer to the Lord and reflecting His love, wisdom, and purpose in every aspect of your life. When approached with a heart tuned to God's will, personal development becomes a powerful act of worship.

From a Christian perspective, it's about transformation—allowing God to shape you to reflect Christ's character. This process not only deepens your relationship with Him, but equips you to fulfill the unique calling He has placed on your life.

Understanding Personal Development

Imagine personal development as a sculptor steadily chipping away at a block of marble to reveal the masterpiece hidden within. The sculptor's vision, patience, and skill bring forth beauty that no one else saw before. In the same way, God is at work in our lives, refining us through circumstances, His Word, and the Holy Spirit's guidance. This process takes time, effort, and a willingness to envision the person God created us to be.

It's not a quick sprint, but a marathon of faith and perseverance. Scripture reminds us in Galatians 6:9 (NIV), *"Let us not become weary in doing good, for at the proper time we will reap a harvest if we do not give up."* Our journey of growth is one of dedication, patience, and openness to change. This path begins with self-awareness—honestly assessing our strengths, weaknesses, passions, and values while inviting the Holy Spirit to guide our understanding of ourselves in light of God's truth.

Asking honest questions—Who am I in Christ? What does God want me to accomplish for His Kingdom? What's holding me back from His best?—lays the foundation for growth. God's Word acts as a mirror, showing us both the beauty of our potential and the areas that need refining. Aligning personal development with your faith ensures that each step forward brings you closer to God's heart and His intended design for your life.

The Importance of Goals

Setting goals is a cornerstone of personal development. Without clear objectives, we risk drifting aimlessly, lacking direction and purpose. Your goals don't need to be extravagant—they just need to matter to you and align with God's will. Perhaps you want to improve communication skills to share the Gospel more effectively, prioritize your health to serve others with renewed energy, or deepen your prayer life to draw closer to the Lord.

Each goal serves as a stepping stone, moving you toward the person God has called you to be. Breaking your goals into smaller, manageable actions helps you stay focused and avoid overwhelm. For instance, if your goal is to strengthen your spiritual walk, start by dedicating a few minutes each morning to prayer and Bible reading. These small, consistent acts of devotion will, over time, lead to significant spiritual growth and prepare you for a greater impact in God's Kingdom. With intentional steps and God's guidance, your goals can become a pathway to fulfilling His purpose for your life.

Overcoming Obstacles

The journey of personal development, much like the journey of faith, is not without its challenges. You may encounter fears, self-doubt, negative habits, or limiting beliefs that seem to stand in the way of your progress. But rather than viewing these obstacles as failures, consider them opportunities for growth and sanctification.

James 1:2-4 (NIV) reminds us: "Consider it pure joy, my brothers and sisters, whenever you face trials of many kinds, because you know that the testing of your faith produces perseverance."

These challenges refine your character, deepen your faith, and strengthen your resolve. Each trial becomes a stepping stone, drawing you closer to the person God created you to be.

Embrace these moments, knowing that God is working through them to shape you for His purpose.

Fear often keeps us locked in our comfort zones, but true growth happens when we step into the unknown, trusting God to guide our steps. Self-doubt whispers, "You're not good enough," yet God's Word boldly declares that you are loved, chosen, and fully equipped for every good work (Ephesians 2:10).

Negative habits and limiting beliefs act like weeds, choking out the growth in your spiritual garden. Removing them requires spiritual discipline, persistent prayer, and replacing lies with the truth found in Scripture.

Rather than letting these hurdles defeat you, face them with courage and faith. Pray for strength and wisdom to navigate the challenges.

Reflect on past victories, recalling how God has faithfully brought you through before. Surround yourself with fellow believers who will encourage and uplift you, reminding you of your God-given worth and limitless potential.

With God's help, you can overcome any obstacle and continue growing into the person He has called you to be.

The Role of Mentorship and Community

Personal development isn't meant to be a solo journey—God designed us for fellowship and mutual encouragement. Hebrews 10:24-25 (NIV) reminds us:

"And let us consider how we may spur one another on toward love and good deeds... encouraging one another."

Mentors, friends, and a Christ-centered community are invaluable as you grow. A mentor provides wisdom and guidance from their own experiences, helping you navigate challenges and recognize opportunities for growth.

Trusted friends offer accountability, celebrate your progress, and stand with you in prayer through struggles.

Engaging in a faith-based community—a small group, Bible study, ministry team, or fellowship gathering—surrounds you with believers who share your values.

These relationships inspire you to keep moving forward, even when the road gets tough. With the support of others, you can grow deeper in your walk with God and stay committed to the goals He's placed on your heart.

Personal Development and Spiritual Growth

For Christians, personal development is deeply connected to spiritual growth. Our aim isn't self-improvement for its own sake, but to better serve God's purposes in our lives. Philippians 1:6 (NIV) reassures us of God's ongoing work: "He who began a good work in you will carry it on to completion until the day of Christ Jesus."

Spiritual maturity involves seeking God's guidance, depending on His strength, and allowing the Holy Spirit to transform you from the inside out. As you draw closer to God through prayer, worship, and studying His Word, the effects become clear. Qualities like peace, patience, kindness, and wisdom begin to influence your decisions, enrich your relationships, and increase your positive impact on others.

When spiritual growth serves as the foundation for personal development, the changes you make go beyond temporary improvements—they carry eternal significance. This alignment ensures that your journey not only reflects God's love but also fulfills His unique purpose for your life. By growing in Christ, you are equipped to live a life of meaning and to shine His light in everything you do.

Practical Steps for Personal Growth

1. **Define Your Vision:** Picture the person God has called you to be. Write down your aspirations, the character traits you want to develop, and the areas where you feel God leading you to grow. This vision provides clarity and direction.

2. **Set Achievable:** Break your vision into smaller, actionable steps. Focus on one or two areas at a time to prevent overwhelm and track your progress. Celebrate small victories along the way.

3. **Embrace Lifelong Learning:** Commit to continuous growth by reading books by Christian authors, listening to sermons and faith-based podcasts, or attending workshops and courses. Learning strengthens your understanding and spiritual disciplines.

4. **Develop Positive Habits:** Lasting change comes from small, consistent actions. Start a morning routine of prayer and Bible study, journal your blessings, or practice daily acts of kindness. These habits shape your character over time.

5. **Seek Feedback:** Be open to feedback from trusted mentors, pastors, or spiritually mature friends. Their honest insights can reveal blind spots and help you refine areas that need growth.

6. **Practice Self-Compassion:** Remember, growth is not always a straight path. Setbacks are opportunities to learn, not failures. Embrace God's grace, knowing His love and forgiveness encourages you to keep moving forward.

By taking these practical steps, you'll align your personal growth with God's purpose, ensuring that every effort is meaningful and impactful for His Kingdom.

The Ripple Effect of Personal Development

As you grow, the blessings of your transformation will extend to your family, friends, church, and community. Your life becomes a living testimony to God's faithfulness and the transformative power of His Spirit. By pursuing personal development rooted in His will, you serve as a beacon of hope, inspiring those around you to seek God's purpose for their own lives.

The ripple effect of your growth is profound. When you live a purposeful, Spirit-filled life, others are naturally drawn to the source of your strength—Jesus Christ. Your choices, words, and actions become a powerful, silent sermon, reflecting Christ's love and inviting others to draw closer to Him. Through your example, lives are touched, hearts are encouraged, and kingdom advances.

Embracing the Journey

The journey of personal development is as valuable as the destination itself. Celebrate every milestone, no matter how small, and take time to recognize God's hand in your progress. Reflect on how far He has brought you and give thanks for the lessons learned along the way.

Remember, growth takes time. It's normal to have moments of doubt or seasons when progress feels slow. What matters most is your commitment to keep moving forward, trusting that God is faithful to complete the good work He has started in you (Philippians 1:6).

Personal development is about living with purpose and fulfillment, becoming the person God designed you to be. By dedicating yourself to this ongoing transformation, you impact not only your own life but also the lives of those around you. It's a journey of faith, taken one step at a time, guided by God's Word and empowered by the Holy Spirit.

Personal Development: An Inspirational Story: Chris Pratt—From Homeless to Hollywood Hero

Consider the story of Chris Pratt, a successful Hollywood actor known for his roles in blockbuster films. His path to stardom wasn't easy. At one point, Pratt experienced homelessness and struggled to find direction.

Although raised in a Christian home, he drifted from the faith and the values he once held dear, becoming lost in the pursuit of success.

A pivotal turning point in Chris Pratt's life came during an unexpected encounter with a stranger named Henry in Hawaii. Sensing a spiritual emptiness that only God could fill, Henry engaged Pratt in a heartfelt conversation, challenging him to examine his priorities and his relationship with God. That moment ignited a deep hunger in Pratt's soul for meaning and purpose that extended far beyond fame or material success.

Pratt's recommitment to Christ became a defining moment, not just for his faith but also for his life as an actor and individual. He took responsibility for his actions, repented of past mistakes, and began to align his personal growth with his renewed faith. His story is a powerful reminder that no matter how far you may wander, it's never too late to return to God and seek His guidance.

As Pratt's career flourished, his faith remained a cornerstone of his life. He publicly acknowledged his dependence on God, often sharing words of wisdom about the power of prayer, perseverance, and faith. He reminded others that these elements, when combined with personal growth, lead to a life of purpose and transformation.

Pratt's journey demonstrates how embracing accountability, leaning into faith, and committing to personal development can bring profound change—not only in one's own life but also in the lives of others inspired by their testimony.

Accountability and Integrity

Pratt's example highlights the importance of staying true to our beliefs and values, even when life's temptations threaten to pull us away. It's easy to pursue dreams and ambitions while neglecting our relationship with God, but his testimony reminds us that it's never too late to turn back, repent, and allow God to reshape our path.

Accountability is key to real personal growth. When you acknowledge your mistakes, repent sincerely, and invite the Holy Spirit to lead your steps, you open the door to true transformation. Taking responsibility for your actions doesn't mean bearing the weight alone—God's grace equips and empowers you to become the person He designed you to be, walking in purpose and fulfillment.

Final Thoughts

Personal development, grounded in a Christian worldview, is about far more than self-improvement—it's about living a life of purpose that aligns with God's will. It's about embracing your identity in Christ, navigating challenges with His strength, and reflecting His light to a world in need of hope and redemption.

By committing to personal growth, you're not only enriching your own life, but also creating a spiritual legacy. Those around you will see God's hand in your journey and be inspired to seek their own transformation. Every step you take is a step of faith, guided by His presence and power.

As you move forward, it's essential to look deeper into your motivations.

In the next chapter, we discuss an important element to our continual growth and success, the development of a 'success mindset'.

CHAPTER 24

DEVELOPING A SUCCESS MINDSET

S uccess is born within the heart and mind before it is ever reflected in external achievements or visible milestones. True success begins with a mindset aligned with God's principles, promises, and purpose. The Bible offers timeless guidance for cultivating this mindset—a success that is rooted in faith, shaped by God's Word, and guided by the Holy Spirit. This isn't about chasing personal ambitions alone, but about living in harmony with God's design for a prosperous and fulfilling life.

In this chapter, we'll explore the transformative journey toward a success mindset through three key steps: **acknowledgment** of God's principles, **acquisition** of His promises, and **alignment** with His will. By examining the lives of biblical figures like Jabez, Joshua, and Peter, we'll uncover how intentional mind renewal and unwavering trust in God can lead to lasting success. Their journeys offer inspiration and practical lessons for aligning our thoughts, decisions, and actions with God's purposes.

Acknowledgment: Recognizing Access to God's Principles and Presence

Transformation begins with acknowledgment. Proverbs 3:6 reminds us: *"In all your ways acknowledge Him, and He shall direct your paths."* (KJV)

Acknowledgment is more than recognizing God's existence; it is an active, intentional choice to invite Him into every area of life. This includes our thoughts, plans, and ambitions. It's a daily act of surrender, where we place our trust in God's infinite wisdom rather than relying on our limited understanding.

When we acknowledge God, we open the door to His presence, guidance, and power. This step requires humility and faith, as we commit to walking in alignment with His principles and allowing Him to lead. Acknowledgment redefines success, shifting our focus from worldly achievements to a heart fully aligned with God's will.

Consider the prayer of Jabez in 1 Chronicles 4:10 (NKJV):

"Oh, that You would bless me indeed, and enlarge my territory, that Your hand would be with me, and that You would keep me from evil."

Jabez's acknowledgment of God as the source of his success and protection set the stage for his transformation. His bold prayer reflected trust in God's ability to bless him abundantly and guide him faithfully. In the same way, our acknowledgment of God invites His hand into our lives, directing our steps and enlarging our capacity for His purposes.

The Foundation for Transformation

Acknowledgment is foundational to cultivating a success mindset. When we consistently recognize God's principles and presence in our lives, we gain clarity, strength, and purpose. This recognition positions us to experience God's guidance, ensuring that our definition of success is rooted in His eternal truths rather than fleeting worldly standards.

From this place of acknowledgment, we are prepared to move into the next stages of transformation: acquiring God's promises and aligning with His will. These steps build upon the foundation of trust and surrender established through acknowledgment, empowering us to live boldly and confidently in the purpose God has designed for us.

The journey toward true success begins with God at the center. As we invite Him into every area of our lives, we find that success is not about what we achieve but about who we become—a reflection of His glory, living out His plans for our good and His Kingdom.

Let's continue this exploration by diving into how we can acquire and act upon God's promises, moving closer to the life He has called us to live.

God's Guidance as Provision

True success begins with God's guidance. It's not merely about external accomplishments, but about aligning our lives with His principles, promises, and purpose. In Joshua 1:8, God gives Joshua a clear directive for achieving success:

"This Book of the Law shall not depart from your mouth, but you shall meditate in it day and night, that you may observe to do according to all that is written in it. For then you will make your way prosperous, and then you will have good success." (NKJV)

This verse highlights the critical role of God's Word in cultivating a success mindset. God's guidance, revealed in His Word and illuminated by the Holy Spirit, is one of His greatest provisions. It directs our paths and aligns our decisions with His perfect will.

The Power of Acknowledging the Holy Spirit

Jesus promised His followers the gift of the Holy Spirit as a teacher, guide, and source of truth:

"But the Helper, the Holy Spirit, whom the Father will send in My name, He

will teach you all things, and bring to your remembrance all things that I said to you." (John 14:26, NKJV)

The Holy Spirit is more than a comforter; He equips us with divine strategies for navigating life's challenges with wisdom. Acknowledging the Spirit's role in our lives opens the door to supernatural insight, empowering us to succeed in ways that go beyond human understanding.

Words as Seeds for Success

From creation, God demonstrated the power of words. In Genesis 1:28, He declared purpose and potential over humanity:

"Be fruitful and multiply; fill the earth and subdue it; have dominion over the fish of the sea, over the birds of the air, and over every living thing that moves on the earth." (NKJV)

These weren't just commands; they were seeds—divine declarations with the power to produce abundance. Similarly, God's Word acts as a seed in our lives. When we meditate on Scripture and declare His promises over our circumstances, we align ourselves with His purpose and position ourselves for success.

God also reaffirmed this principle after the flood:

"While the earth remains, seedtime and harvest, cold and heat, winter and summer, and day and night shall not cease." (Genesis 8:22, NKJV)

This timeless principle reminds us that success grows from the seeds of His Word, planted in our hearts and nurtured through faith.

Acquisition: Replacing the Old to Embrace the New

Transformation requires more than recognition; it demands action. Developing a success mindset involves replacing limiting thoughts, beliefs, and habits with new ones rooted in God's truth. Romans 12:2 emphasizes this process:

"And do not be conformed to this world, but be transformed by the renewing of your mind, that you may prove what is that good and acceptable and perfect will of God." (NKJV)

Jabez: Breaking Free from Limitation

Jabez's story is a powerful example of breaking free from limiting beliefs. His name, meaning "sorrow" or "one who causes pain," defined his identity and constrained his potential. But in 1 Chronicles 4:9-10, Jabez prayed a bold prayer that changed everything:

"Oh, that You would bless me indeed, and enlarge my territory, that Your hand would be with me, and that You would keep me from evil, that I may not cause pain!" (NKJV)

This prayer marked a turning point in Jabez's life. By rejecting the limitations of his name and embracing the blessings of the Abrahamic Covenant, Jabez repositioned himself for expansion and success.

Peter: Replacing Guilt with Vision

Peter's transformation shows how God's grace replaces shame with purpose. After Peter denied Jesus three times, he was overwhelmed with guilt. Yet, in John 21:15-17, Jesus restored Peter by asking him three times, "Do you love Me?"

Each affirmation of love replaced the painful memory of denial with renewed purpose. Jesus then commissioned Peter to shepherd His people, reminding us that God's grace empowers us to move beyond failure and embrace His calling.

This process teaches us the importance of actively displacing old, harmful thoughts with new, empowering ones rooted in God's truth. Just as Peter envisioned himself fulfilling Christ's commission, we too must replace limiting beliefs with God's promises.

The Power of Visualization

Renewing the mind involves more than replacing old thoughts; it requires visualizing the life God has planned for us. Like Jabez, who saw himself blessed, and Peter, who envisioned himself fulfilling Christ's mission, we too must align our mental image with God's vision. Visualization is a powerful tool for replacing worldly blueprints with His divine design.

Alignment: Living in Agreement with God's Principles

A success mindset is not just about acquiring new beliefs—it's about aligning every part of our lives with God's principles. Joshua 1:8 emphasizes the importance of consistency:

"This Book of the Law shall not depart from your mouth, but you shall meditate in it day and night, that you may observe to do according to all that is written in it. For then you will make your way prosperous, and then you will have good success." (NKJV)

Abiding in the Word

Jesus reinforces this principle in John 15:7:

"If you abide in Me, and My words abide in you, you will ask what you desire, and it shall be done for you." (NKJV)

Abiding in Christ means letting His Word shape our thoughts, guide our actions, and direct our decisions. This deep connection nourishes our spirits and produces the fruit of true success.

Overcoming Obstacles to Alignment

To align with God's principles, we must remove obstacles that hinder growth, such as:

- **Negative Self-Talk:** Replace thoughts of inadequacy with declarations of God's promises.

- **Worldly Perspectives:** Reject cultural messages that conflict with Scripture.

- **Unhealed Wounds:** Seek God's healing to overcome past hurts and step into freedom.

Alignment is an ongoing process that requires intentionality, humility, and perseverance.

Abundance: Experiencing God's Promises

God's desire for us goes beyond survival; He calls us to live in abundance. Psalm 35:27 declares:

"Let the Lord be magnified, who has pleasure in the prosperity of His servant." (NKJV)

As heirs to the promises of the Abrahamic Covenant through Christ, we are entitled to blessings of provision, protection, and purpose:

"And if you are Christ's, then you are Abraham's seed, and heirs according to the promise." (Galatians 3:29, NKJV)

Conclusion

Developing a success mindset is not about chasing worldly recognition but about embracing God's purpose. By acknowledging His presence, acquiring His promises, aligning with His principles, and stepping into His abundance, we position ourselves for transformation and fulfillment.

The lives of Jabez, Joshua, and Peter remind us that success begins within—a heart surrendered to God, a mind renewed by His Word, and a spirit guided by His truth. No matter where you start, God's promises are available to those who seek Him with faith and humility.

Prayer for a Success Mindset

The journey to developing a success mindset begins with transformation—a renewal of the mind and heart that aligns us with God's promises and purpose. As we meditate on His Word and seek His guidance, we open ourselves to the abundant blessings He has prepared for us. Transformation is not achieved through human effort alone but through surrendering to God's wisdom, trusting in His provision, and allowing His Spirit to lead us.

This prayer is an invitation for God to work within us, to replace limiting beliefs with His truth, and to expand our vision to match His divine plan. It reflects the bold faith of Jabez, the commitment of Joshua, and the restoration of Peter—reminding us that God's presence and guidance are the foundation for true success. As you pray, let your heart be open to the transformation God desires to bring into your life, and trust in His ability to lead you into a future filled with purpose and prosperity.

Heavenly Father,

I surrender my mind, heart, and soul to You completely. Transform me by the renewing of my mind, replacing every limiting belief, every doubt, and every fear with the unshakable truth of Your Word. Let my thoughts align with Your thoughts and my desires with Your will. Help me to meditate deeply on Your promises, letting Your Word take root in my heart and shape my actions daily.

Lord, I acknowledge Your presence in every area of my life—my decisions, relationships, and dreams—and I invite You to lead me with Your divine wisdom. Teach me to walk in step with Your principles, embracing Your love and truth as the foundation of all I do.

Holy Spirit, I ask for Your guidance in every choice I make. Empower me with courage and strength to trust Your leading, even when the path seems uncertain. Let me embrace the abundant blessings You have prepared for me with a heart full of gratitude and faith.

Father, may my life be a living testimony of Your grace, reflecting Your glory and fulfilling the unique purpose You have designed for me. Use me as a vessel to bring light and hope to others, demonstrating the joy and peace found in walking with You.

Thank You for Your unending love, Your faithfulness, and the gift of transformation through Christ. I surrender everything to You, trusting that Your plans for me are good and perfect. In Jesus' mighty name, I pray, Amen.

Now that we've discussed the importance of development a success mindset, it's time to focus on another vital element that will prepare you to fully step into your God-given potential. Let's explore this next foundational piece of the journey. **Know Your Why.**

CHAPTER 25

UNDERSTANDING YOUR "WHY": THE FOUNDATION FOR PURPOSEFUL LIVING

Every great journey begins with a God-given purpose. Whether pursuing personal transformation, professional ambition, or a spiritual calling, uncovering your "why" unlocks your potential and propels you to fulfill God's plan for your life.

Your "why" goes beyond setting goals; it's the deep motivation that fuels your passion and anchors you during life's storms. It keeps you steadfast when trials arise and distractions threaten to derail you. Knowing your "why" connects you to God's eternal purpose, giving meaning to even the smallest acts of obedience. When aligned with His will, these moments of faith can transform your life and the lives of those around you."

The Importance of Knowing Your "Why"

Your "why" serves as a spiritual compass, constantly pointing you back to God's will. It provides clarity and direction when doubts, temptations, or challenges arise. But discovering this divine purpose isn't automatic—it requires intentional effort. Through sincere prayer, honest self-reflection, and seeking God's guidance, you can begin to uncover the deeper motivations He has placed in your heart.

The journey to uncover your "why" may be challenging, but it is profoundly rewarding. Knowing your 'why' is critical. A clear "why" takes you beyond surface-level ambitions, rooting your life in God's truth and aligning your heart with His purpose.

What Is Your "Why"?

At its core, your "why" is your reason for being—the God-given purpose that shapes your decisions, actions, and priorities. It drives you to rise each morning, even when the path ahead feels uncertain or overwhelming.

Without a clear "why," it's easy to feel adrift, discouraged, or tempted to give up when faced with difficulties. However, when your purpose is grounded in God's eternal truth, every trial becomes an opportunity for growth, and every victory holds eternal significance.

Faith Empowered By Purpose

When you understand your "why," your faith is empowered with greater conviction. Throughout scripture, great figures of faith found their "why" in God's calling, which enabled them to persevere and achieve extraordinary things.

Moses: Finding Courage in Calling

Moses fled Egypt in fear and spent 40 years in exile. But at the burning bush, he encountered his "why"—to deliver God's people from bondage.

This divine purpose reignited his courage and reshaped his identity. With unwavering faith, Moses stood before Pharaoh and fulfilled God's call to lead Israel to freedom.

Esther: A Time Such as This

Queen Esther's "why" was rooted in God's providence. She risked her life to save her people, declaring, "If I perish, I perish" (Esther 4:16). Her courage, driven by purpose, not only preserved the Jewish people, but also demonstrated the power of trusting God's plan.

Esther's actions illustrate the strength of aligning with God's purpose, even at the risk of personal safety. Esther saw her role as queen as a divine appointment that allowed her to advocate for her people. Her willingness to embrace her God-given role, even in the face of fear and uncertainty, serves as a timeless reminder that God equips and empowers us to fulfill His purpose.

David: Defending God's Honor

As a young shepherd, David faced Goliath, a giant far stronger and more experienced. But David's "why" was clear: to defend God's honor. His love for God and sense of purpose emboldened him to defeat Goliath, securing victory for Israel and demonstrating the power of faith-driven courage.

Discover Your "Why"

Ask yourself: What truly motivates you? Is it a desire to honor God, provide for your family, serve your community, or share the gospel with those who do not know Christ?

Knowing your "why" centers your heart on what truly matters and empowers you to keep going when challenges arise. Your "why" transforms your work, relationships, and daily routines into acts of worship.

A Compass For The Journey

Life is filled with distractions and challenges that can lead you astray. Your "why" acts as a filter, helping you invest your time, energy, and resources wisely for God's Kingdom. It keeps you focused, fuels your perseverance, and shapes your character in ways that honor God.

Philippians 1:6 (NIV) reassures us:

"He who began a good work in you will carry it on to completion until the day of Christ Jesus."

Trust that the God who planted your "why" in your heart is faithful to sustain it. He will guide you every step of the way, providing strength when you're weary and grace when the path feels steep.

The Transformation Ahead

Living out your "why" often requires a deeper transformation—reshaping not just your actions but also your heart and mind. As I mentioned earlier in this book, this process mirrors one of nature's most profound changes: the metamorphosis of a caterpillar into a butterfly.

In the next chapter, we'll explore Part 2 of "Metamorphosis: The Parallel Between a Caterpillar, a Butterfly, and Believers." Just as the caterpillar enters a cocoon for unseen growth and preparation, we too experience hidden seasons where God works to mold us into His image and prepare us for a greater purpose.

Let's dive into this remarkable parallel and discover how embracing the process of transformation leads to the fullness of life God has designed for you.

CHAPTER 26

METAMORPHOSIS: THE PARALLEL BETWEEN A CATAPILLA, A BUTTERFLY AND BELIEVERS - PT. 2

In Part 1, I gave an analogy comparing the transformation of a caterpillar into a butterfly to the journey of believers. It's interesting how people often dismiss the idea of being likened to a caterpillar—a lowly worm—yet eagerly embrace comparisons to a beautiful butterfly. What many overlook is that the butterfly is simply a caterpillar that has undergone a remarkable process of transformation.

This comparison also applies to the lives of successful people. Many admire their achievements and wish they could trade places with them, but they fail to see or appreciate the struggles and growth these individuals endured during their "chrysalis state." Success is rarely glamorous in its early stages. It's forged in seasons of challenge, perseverance, and transformation—hidden from the eyes of others.

In the first part of this analogy, we compared the beginning of the transformational journey of a believer to that of a caterpillar navigating its initial stages.

Now, we move into the second phase, where the miracle of transformation takes place. Just as a caterpillar enters a cocoon for its metamorphosis—a time of hidden changes—we also experience seasons of growth that may not be visible to those around us. These moments of quiet surrender and deep inner work are where we undergo transformation, even when we cannot yet see the results.

Hidden Transformation: The Cocoon and the Christian Journey

Imagine a tiny caterpillar, seemingly ordinary and limited, confined to crawling and consuming. Its entire existence appears defined by its current state—until the moment of transformation begins. The cocoon is not a place of death, but a miraculous workshop of divine redesign.

Inside the cocoon, everything changes. The old structures literally dissolve. Cells break down, reorganize, and reimagine themselves. Isn't this exactly what happens in our spiritual walk? Paul understood this deeply when he wrote about becoming a "new creation." It's not cosmetic change—it's fundamental reconstruction.

Just as the caterpillar doesn't resist its metamorphosis, true Christian transformation requires surrender. It's not about trying harder, but about yielding completely.

The cocoon represents that sacred space between who you were and who you're becoming—a protective cocoon where God does His most intimate work.

Three Profound Spiritual Truths from Caterpillar Metamorphosis:

1. Transformation Requires Stillness

The caterpillar doesn't fight the process or try to rush its development. It simply rests and allows the transformation to happen. How often do we resist God's work in us by trying to control or speed up the outcome?

Transformation requires stillness—not the absence of action, but a steadfastness of faith in the face of turmoil and struggles. This kind of stillness means holding your ground, trusting God's promises, and refusing to be swayed by fear or doubt.

When Moses stood before the Red Sea with the Israelites trapped between Pharaoh's army and the water, he delivered a powerful instruction: "Stand still, and see the salvation of the Lord." (Exodus 14:13)

It was in their calmness—anchored in faith—that the Israelites experienced God's miraculous deliverance. Their fear of the advancing Egyptian army made them cry out in terror. However, by following Moses' instruction to 'stand still'—to remain steadfast in their faith in God—they found inner peace and confidence as they walked on dry ground through the Red Sea, which God had opened for them.

In the same way, our journey of transformation calls for this unwavering trust. The obstacles and struggles we encounter are not meant to defeat us, but to deepen our reliance on God.

When we hold our position of faith, we will see His salvation, His deliverance, and His power at work in our lives.

True transformation happens when we trust God to carry us through the challenges, believing He is faithful to complete the work He has begun in us.

2. Unseen Doesn't Mean Unimportant

Most of the miracle happens where no one can see—in the quiet, hidden places of your life. Just like seeds grow beneath the soil before sprouting, your most significant spiritual work often takes place out of sight, unnoticed by the outside world.

But don't underestimate these unseen moments. It's in these times of quiet surrender, prayer, and obedience that transformation truly begins. Though invisible to others, this work is laying the foundation for the visible changes that will one day reflect God's power and grace in your life.

3. Struggles That Strengthen

 The butterfly's emergence from the cocoon is a struggle. Without the resistance and effort involved in breaking free, its wings would remain weak, unable to lift it into flight. In the same way, the challenges we face—our trials, conflicts, and faith struggles—are not wasted. They equip us with endurance and spiritual fortitude. James 1:2–4 reassures us that these trials produce perseverance, ultimately leading us toward maturity and completeness.

We may wonder why transformation sometimes feels painful, but just as the butterfly must fight to unfold its wings, believers must learn resilience to fulfill God's call on their lives.

Pain Precedes Breakthrough

When the butterfly finally breaks free, it is unrecognizable from its former self. Its delicate, colorful wings, a transformed perspective, and a renewed purpose showcase the beauty of complete metamorphosis.

This awe-inspiring natural process mirrors what Spirit-led transformation looks like in our lives.

Just as the butterfly gains the ability to soar, we, too, are equipped with new strengths and spiritual gifts as we are transformed. Through this renewal, we rise above old limitations and begin to see life from God's perspective. Transformation isn't just about outward change—it's a complete re-creation of who we are, touching every part of our existence and aligning us with God's purpose.

The butterfly's emergence teaches us several vital truths about spiritual transformation:

1. **Embrace Your New Identity**

   Your transformation isn't just about doing different things; it's about becoming who God designed you to be. Like the butterfly that naturally knows how to spread its wings, your new identity comes with divine instincts. You don't need to strive or force yourself into your calling - it flows naturally from who you've become.

2. **Rising to a New Perspective**

Once liberated, the butterfly sees the world from an entirely different vantage point—a panoramic view from above rather than ground level. For Christians who have embraced their new identity in Christ, the Holy Spirit grants an elevated perspective: we begin to see life's struggles, relationships, and even our purpose through spiritual eyes. Paul encouraged believers to "seek those things which are above, where Christ is" (Colossians 3:1). This higher view enables us to discern God's will and to live by faith rather than by sight, understanding that our ultimate citizenship is in heaven.

1. Fulfill Your Divine Purpose. Every butterfly's unique patterns and colors serve a role in nature's grand design. Similarly, your transformation equips you with specific gifts and abilities to fulfill your unique purpose in God's kingdom. What you've become is essential to His plan, and no one else can accomplish what you're designed to do.

Living as a Transformed Being

Living transformed means walking in newfound authority while staying humble, exercising spiritual gifts, while remaining dependent on the Holy Spirit, and using your testimony to inspire others. The butterfly doesn't need to prove its transformation; its very existence testifies to the miracle that occurred.

When the Holy Spirit transforms us, we become living proof of His power. Our lives demonstrate that with God, breakthrough is possible, limitation gives way to liberation, and the impossible becomes possible. Transformation isn't about merely surviving—it's about soaring.

Remember, this stage of transformation is not the end of your journey; it's the beginning of living out your true purpose. Like the butterfly strengthening its wings before flight, you, too, will grow stronger as you embrace your new identity.

Metamorphosis: The Transformation Of A Catapilla To A Butterfly

This powerful demonstration of transformation in nature reminds us that change is not only possible but essential for our growth as believers who are being shaped into the image of Christ.

2 Corinthians 3:18 "And we all, who with unveiled faces contemplate the Lord's glory, are being transformed into his (Christ) image with ever-increasing glory, which comes from the Lord, who is the Spirit." This verse highlights how the Holy Spirit continually works to transform believers, shaping them to reflect the character and likeness of Christ more and more.

Like the caterpillar, we are called to embrace the process of change, trusting that what may seem hidden or uncomfortable is preparing us for something greater.

This transformation leads us to **The Journey to Your Best Self**, where the work of renewal unfolds, and we begin to step fully into the person

God created us to be. Just as the butterfly emerges with wings to fulfill its purpose, so, too, are we empowered to live boldly and abundantly when we allow God to shape us.

Now, let's proceed to the topic of 'the journey to your best self', where we will learn how to partner with God to reach our fullest potential.

CHAPTER 27

THE TRIFECTA OF TRANSFORMATION: DESIRE, DECISION, AND DISCIPLINE

Transformation doesn't happen by accident. It requires intentionality, persistence, and a willingness to embrace challenges. At the heart of meaningful and lasting change is a powerful trio: **desire**, **decision**, and **discipline**. These three elements work together to propel you toward your God-given purpose.

- **Desire** sparks the journey—it's the yearning that awakens your vision for something greater.

- **Decision** turns that spark into a flame by transforming desire into clear, deliberate action.

- **Discipline** sustains the flame, empowering you to persevere through trials and distractions.

When this trifecta operates in harmony, it aligns your life with God's plan, fuels your growth, and helps you reach your full potential. Let's explore each element and reflect on how they shape your transformation journey.

The Foundation Of Desire

Desire is the starting point of every significant accomplishment. It begins as a faint stirring in your heart—a longing for something better. It could be a desire to grow closer to God, mend a relationship, or pursue a long-held dream.

The Origin of Desire

Desires can be God-given or self-centered. Psalm 37:4 teaches us, *"Delight yourself in the Lord, and He will give you the desires of your heart."* When we align ourselves with God, He refines our desires to match His will. God-given desires inspire purpose, fulfillment, and growth, while self-centered desires often lead to frustration and regret.

Consider Nehemiah. His desire to rebuild Jerusalem's walls began as a burden in his heart. This God-inspired desire led him to seek the Lord, take bold action, and persevere despite opposition (Nehemiah 1–6). Nehemiah's story demonstrates how a God-aligned desire can have monumental impact when paired with decision and discipline.

Cultivating Godly Desires

To ensure your desires honor God, ask yourself:

- Does this desire glorify God?

- Will pursuing this desire draw me closer to His purpose?

- Am I willing to surrender this desire if it conflicts with His will?

Godly desires align with His Word, inspire growth, and steer you toward His best. Cultivate these desires through prayer, immersing yourself in Scripture, and staying sensitive to the Holy Spirit's guidance.

Decision: Fueling the Flame

Desire may ignite the flame, but **decision** fuels it. A decision is the moment you commit to pursuing your desire, regardless of the obstacles ahead. It's the turning point where wishful thinking becomes purposeful action.

The Weight of a Single Decision

Decisions shape your destiny. Joshua's challenge to the Israelites— *"Choose this day whom you will serve"* (Joshua 24:15)—underscored the life-defining power of choice. Similarly, the prodigal son's restoration began with a single decision: *"I will arise and go to my father"* (Luke 15:18).

Even the smallest decision can change your trajectory when it aligns with God's will.

Overcoming Barriers to Decisiveness

Many people get stuck between desire and action due to fear, doubt, or indecision. Common barriers include:

- **Fear of Failure**: What if I make the wrong choice?

- **Perfectionism**: Waiting for the "perfect" moment.

- **Comfort Zones**: Avoiding the discomfort of change.

To overcome these barriers, remember that indecision is a decision in itself—a decision to stay stagnant. Trust God to guide you. Proverbs 3:5-6 reminds us to "Trust in the Lord with all your heart, and He will make straight your paths."

Making Firm Decisions

A firm decision is rooted in conviction and aligned with your values. To make effective decisions:

1. **Seek God's Guidance**: Pray for wisdom (James 1:5).

2. **Clarify Your Priorities**: Ensure your decision aligns with your goals and purpose.

3. **Act Boldly**: Once you've made a decision, commit fully. Half-hearted decisions lead to half-hearted results.

Discipline: Turning Intentions Into Reality

While desire and decision set the stage, **discipline** keeps you moving forward. Discipline bridges the gap between intention and accomplishment. It's the daily choice to stay the course, even when the road gets tough.

What is Discipline?

Nick Saban, a celebrated football coach, defines discipline as "doing what you're supposed to do, when you're supposed to do it, the way it's supposed to be done." It is the ability to prioritize long-term rewards over short-term comfort.

The Apostle Paul highlights discipline in 1 Corinthians 9:25-27: "Everyone who competes in the games goes into strict training... I strike a blow to my body and make it my slave so that after I have preached to others, I myself will not be disqualified for the prize." Discipline is the practice of training yourself to consistently pursue what matters most.

Discipline in Action

Discipline manifests in two ways:

1. **Doing What You Should Do, Even When You Don't Feel Like It**

   This includes maintaining commitments, completing tasks, and persevering through challenges. For example, waking early for prayer or study requires discipline, but the spiritual growth it fosters is invaluable.

2. **Avoiding What You Shouldn't Do, Even When You Want To**

   Discipline also involves resisting temptation and saying "no" to distractions. Jesus exemplified this in the wilderness when He resisted Satan's temptations, choosing obedience to God over immediate gratification (Matthew 4:1-11).

The Role of the Holy Spirit

Discipline isn't just self-will; it's Spirit-empowered. Galatians 5:22–23 reminds us that self-control is a fruit of the Spirit. Rely on God's strength to sustain you when your own resolve falters.

When Desire, Decision, and Discipline Align

When these three elements work together, they create a powerful synergy:

1. **Desire** provides the "why"—the motivation to pursue a goal.

2. **Decision** provides the "what"—a commitment to act.

3. **Discipline** provides the "how"—the consistent effort to stay the course.

Biblical Examples

- **Nehemiah**: His desire to rebuild Jerusalem's walls led to decisive action and unwavering discipline, even in the face of opposition.

- **Ruth**: Her desire to stay with Naomi, her decision to follow Naomi's God, and her discipline in working diligently in the fields led to God's blessing and her role in the lineage of Christ.

- **Paul**: His desire to spread the Gospel, his decision to follow Christ, and his disciplined ministry changed the course of history.

The Reward of Alignment

When desire, decision, and discipline work together, the rewards are abundant:

- **Personal Growth**: You become more resilient, focused, and purposeful.

- **Spiritual Maturity**: Your walk with God deepens as you align your actions with His will.

- **Fulfillment**: Achieving goals and living in obedience to God brings lasting satisfaction.

James 1:12 says, "Blessed is the one who perseveres under trial because, having stood the test, that person will receive the crown of life that the Lord has promised to those who love Him." Perseverance fueled by desire, decision, and discipline leads to eternal rewards.

A CALL TO ACTION

Take a moment to reflect:

- What desires has God placed in your heart?

- What decisions do you need to make to move toward those desires?

- How can you grow in discipline to stay the course?

Ask the Holy Spirit to guide you and take the next step in faith. Transformation is a journey, not a one-time event. Each step, fueled by desire, decision, and discipline, brings you closer to becoming the person God created you to be.

True change doesn't happen by chance. It requires intentional effort, determination, and the courage to face challenges. Desire ignites your passion, decision sets your direction, and discipline keeps you moving forward—all working together to align you with God's plan.

As we look ahead, this next chapter is not just about reaching our goals; it's also about evolving into the individuals that God intended us to be. Let's confidently embrace His purpose together, trusting the Holy Spirit to guide and support us on our journey.

CHAPTER 28

THE JOURNEY TO YOUR BEST SELF

As we near the conclusion of *"Transformation: Change Begins With-in—The Journey to Your Best Self,"* let's reflect on what it truly means to pursue becoming your best self.

In this context, your "best self" is not about perfection in human terms but about becoming the person God created you to be and living the life He designed, aligned with His purpose and plan.

From the outset, it's important to recognize that this journey is ongoing—a process that continues until Christ returns and perfects us. The Apostle Paul reassures us of this truth in Philippians 1:6 (AMP):

"I am convinced and confident of this very thing, that He who has begun a good work in you will [continue to] perfect and complete it until the day of Christ Jesus [the time of His return]."

This verse reminds us that while we strive to grow and transform, the ultimate work of perfection belongs to God. He is faithful to complete what He started in you, and your role is to embrace the process and trust His guidance.

God's Purpose For You: Discovering Your Calling

Ephesians 2:10 (NIV) declares:

"For we are God's handiwork, created in Christ Jesus to do good works, which God prepared in advance for us to do."

You were created with a divine purpose—to glorify God and serve others. This purpose may unfold in the spiritual or secular realm, but it always aligns with God's plan for your life. Many believers wrestle with the question:

"How do I find my purpose?"

The answer often lies in the process of discovery. Purpose isn't always a single defining task; it frequently reveals itself through a series of smaller assignments. Each step of faithful obedience builds toward a greater calling. As you walk with God, He equips you with the skills, talents, and passions needed to fulfill your purpose. When you align your natural gifts with His direction, you move closer to becoming the person He designed you to be.

The Identity Challenge: Understanding Who You Are

To step into your best self, you must first know who you are in Christ. Without clarity in your identity, navigating life's challenges and fulfilling your calling becomes difficult.

Genesis 1:27 tells us:

"So God created mankind in His own image, in the image of God He created them; male and female He created them."

Your value and worth come from being made in His image. While your family, culture, and experiences shape aspects of your earthly identity, your ultimate identity is rooted in Christ. Ephesians 1:13-14 affirms that you are sealed in Him, chosen and redeemed.

But let's be honest—have you ever felt like you were wearing a mask, pretending to be someone else to meet others' expectations? This disconnect often leads to an identity crisis. Many people conform to worldly standards, losing sight of who they are in Christ.

However, the journey to reclaim your true identity begins with Scripture.

Psalm 139:23-24 offers a powerful prayer for self-discovery:

"Search me, God, and know my heart; test me and know my anxious thoughts. See if there is any offensive way in me, and lead me in the way everlasting."

By inviting God to reveal your heart, you begin peeling back layers of false identities to uncover your authentic self. Transformation into His image is a gradual process led by the Holy Spirit (2 Corinthians 3:18).

The Spirit provides clarity, guidance, and grace, empowering you to embrace who you are in Christ.

Living From Identity, Not For Identity

1. The Problem: Striving for Identity

Many believers feel the need to *earn* their identity or self-worth by achieving success, gaining approval, or meeting worldly standards. This leads to a cycle of striving—working hard to prove value through titles, accomplishments, or the praise of others.

The danger here is that identity becomes performance-based, fragile, and conditional. When success fades or approval is loss, their sense of self crumbles.

From a biblical standpoint, this mindset reflects the world's system, which often ties value to *doing* rather than *being*. However, this is contrary to the way God views and defines us.

- **Romans 8:15-16 (NKJV):**

  "For you did not receive the spirit of bondage again to fear, but you received the Spirit of adoption by whom we cry out, 'Abba, Father.' The Spirit Himself bears witness with our spirit that we are children of God."

Our identity is not earned; it is given. As children of God, our worth comes from our relationship with Him, not from our performance.

This truth transforms how you live:

- **Your identity is received, not achieved.**

- **You serve God from acceptance, not for acceptance.**

- **Your worth is defined by your relationship with Him, not your performance.**

The Holy Spirit is your divine coach on this journey. He reminds you of your adoption (Romans 8:16), reveals your inheritance in Christ (1 Corinthians 2:12), and renews your mind to think in alignment with your true identity (Romans 12:2). With His guidance, you gain confidence, humility, and purpose without striving for perfection.

Overcoming Obstacles And Walking In Purpose

The enemy often attacks your identity because he knows a believer secure in their identity is a threat to his plans. But the Holy Spirit equips you to stand firm:

- **With truth to combat lies** (John 8:32)

- **With peace to silence, doubts** (Philippians 4:7)

- **With power to live boldly** (2 Timothy 1:7)

As you embrace your identity and purpose, you begin to live authentically and confidently as the person God created you to be.

This transformation touches every area of your life—your relationships, your work, and your faith. It allows you to impact others in profound ways, fulfilling not just your calling but also advancing His Kingdom.

Discovering Your Identity and Purpose

When you understand who you truly are and the purpose you were created for, you can live your best life.

By recognizing your unique strengths and allowing God to guide your journey, you begin a path that not only fulfills your potential but also leaves a positive impact on the people around you.

As you take this journey of self-discovery and growth, real change starts to happen. This brings us to the heart of the discussion...

Transformation: A Journey of Change

In this final chapter, we'll explore how the changes you've made inside yourself lead to lasting growth. These changes help you become the best version of yourself and inspire you to make a difference in the world.

CHAPTER 29

TRANSFORMATION: YOUR JOURNEY TO A NEW YOU

Before stepping into your new chapter, pause and acknowledge your progress. This journey of transformation hasn't been easy, but every step you've taken has brought you closer to becoming the person you were meant to be. The changes you've made inside yourself—your mindset, habits, and values—have not only reshaped your life, but also prepared you to inspire and impact the world around you.

The Power of Internal Change

True transformation begins within. It starts with recognizing the areas of your life that needed growth and taking intentional steps to address them. By shifting your perspective and embracing a mindset of possibility, you've unlocked the potential to overcome challenges that once seemed insurmountable.

Each change you've made—whether it was releasing past hurts, breaking free from limiting beliefs, or committing to personal growth—has created a ripple effect in your life. Like a seed planted in fertile soil, the work you've done inside is beginning to bear fruit. You are no longer defined by your past, but by the hope and vision you have for your future.

Becoming the Best Version of Yourself

The path to a new version of yourself involves evolving into your optimal self, focusing on continuous improvement instead of perfection. It's about living authentically, aligned with your values, and true to your purpose.

You've learned that growth isn't a destination but a continuous process, one that invites you to keep learning, evolving, and striving toward excellence.

As you've embraced this journey, you've discovered strengths you didn't know you had. You've faced fears, taken risks, and pushed beyond your comfort zone.

These steps have built resilience and confidence, empowering you to approach life with boldness and clarity. You are living proof that change is not only possible but also powerful.

Making a Difference in the World

Transformation isn't just about personal growth; it's about how your growth impacts others. As you've become stronger and more self-aware, your ability to positively influence those around you has grown. Your story, your journey, and your example are now a source of inspiration for others who may be walking a similar path.

Think of the relationships you've strengthened, the kindness you've shown, and the encouragement you've offered. Every small action creates a ripple effect that reaches further than you might imagine. By sharing your authentic self with the world, you are making a meaningful difference.

The Road Ahead

As you move forward, remember that the journey doesn't end here. Life will continue to bring new challenges and opportunities for growth.

Embrace them with the same courage and determination that brought you to this point. Keep seeking ways to grow, learn, and contribute, and never underestimate the power of your influence.

Surround yourself with people who uplift and inspire you. Continue to nurture the habits and practices that have brought you success.

Most importantly, stay true to your purpose and values, allowing them to guide your decisions and actions.

A Final Thought

Your transformation is more than achieving a goal; Each day, you have the opportunity to step into your potential and live a life of meaning and fulfillment.

The changes you've made inside yourself are the foundation for lasting growth, enabling you to face the future with hope, strength, and confidence.

As you move ahead, keep in mind that transformation is a gift, benefiting not only yourself but also the world. By becoming your best self, you inspire others to do the same.

You leave a legacy of growth, kindness, and lasting impact.

Welcome to the new you. The best is yet to come.

A Closing Prayer

As we come to the end of this moment together, let us pause to reflect on all that we've shared and to thank God for His presence with us. We are grateful for the wisdom and insight He has given, the peace that has filled our hearts, and the strength He continues to provide.

This is a time to express our gratitude to Him for His faithfulness, for the lessons we've learned, and for the work He is doing in our lives. Let's join together in prayer, thanking God for His goodness and asking Him to guide us as we move forward. Let us pray.

Dear Heavenly Father,

We come before You with hearts full of gratitude. Thank You for Your presence with us during this time and for the wisdom, encouragement, and truth You have revealed. We are so grateful for the love and grace You continually pour into our lives.

As we leave this place, we ask for Your guidance and strength to carry what we have learned into our daily lives. Help us to walk in Your purpose, to reflect Your light, and to be a blessing to those around us. Fill us with Your peace, and let Your Spirit lead us in all that we do.

Lord, we thank You for Your faithfulness, for always meeting us where we are and transforming us into who You've called us to be. May the seeds You've planted in our hearts today take root and grow, bearing fruit for Your glory.

Go with us now, Father, and keep us close to You. May we continue to seek Your will and trust in Your plan as we move forward in faith.

In Jesus' name, we pray. Amen.

ACKNOWLEDGEMENTS

I want to express my love and gratitude to my wife, Pat, for her unwavering love, encouragement, and steadfast support throughout the writing of this book. You have been my rock, my partner, and my inspiration every step of the way, and I am eternally grateful for you.

A special thanks to my children—Darius, Dereik, LaKisha, Jerriel, and Tommy—for your love, support, and belief in me. Each of you brings joy and strength to my life, and your encouragement has been a source of motivation and pride.

To the members and supporters of Faith Clinic Christian Center, my heartfelt thanks to each of you for your prayers, encouragement, and unwavering faith in this mission. Your support has been invaluable, and this book came to fruition with you by my side.

To all who have walked this journey with me—thank you for being part of my life and for inspiring me to give my best in everything I do.

I am deeply grateful.

With love and appreciation,

D. Lee A, Simpson

CONNECT WITH THE AUTHOR

Grace and peace to you! Thank you for reading my book and allowing my words to be a part of your spiritual journey. I am deeply grateful for your support and would love to continue walking alongside you in faith. Whether you have prayers to share, questions about the book, or simply wish to connect, please reach out through the platforms below.

Let's grow together in Christ's love!

FACEBOOK

https://www.facebook.com/DrLeeSimpson

TWITTER

@drLSimpson

https://twitter.com/drLSimpson

EMAIL: Lifebooks@dlscreativeworks.com

Website Link For Books By Dr. Lee A. Simpson